☆ ☆ ☆ ☆ ☆ ☆ ☆ ☆ ☆ ☆ ☆

Americans At War

☆ ☆ ☆ ☆ ☆ ☆ ☆ ☆ ☆ ☆ ☆

T. Harry Williams

AMERICANS AT WAR

The Development
of the American Military System

LOUISIANA STATE UNIVERSITY PRESS

☆ ☆ ☆ ☆ ☆ ☆ ☆ ☆ ☆ ☆ ☆

TO

Troy H. Middleton

A Soldier of the Republic

Author's Preface

THE FOLLOWING essays on the American military system were delivered as the J. P. Young Lectures in American history at Memphis State University in October, 1956. The term essay is deliberately used, because nobody could be more aware than the author of the tentative nature of some of the findings and opinions here presented. Although the lectures represent the result of years of teaching and studying military history, they are necessarily, in certain sections, speculative and open to revision. And this is because the history of war has been, until recent times, a neglected subject in our national record. We need urgently a study, or a series of studies, of the American military organization in the nineteenth century, of command arrangements in war and peace, and of the factors that determined the framing of strategic decisions. If these essays, by provoking dissent or correction, should help to bring about such a consummation, the author will feel amply rewarded. He wishes to make one more self-protecting qualification.

He is well aware that in discussing our military system he has devoted primary attention to the army. This is not because he is unaware of the contributions of the navy in our wars, but rather because his researches in military history have centered around the development and the doings of the land forces.

For permission to quote material, due acknowledgment is made to the following: The Macmillan Company for Leonard White, *The Jeffersonians* and *The Jacksonians*; Houghton Mifflin Company for Frederic L. Paxson, *America at War, 1917–1918*; Harvard University Press for Elihu Root, *The Military and Colonial Policy of the United States*; and to Alvin Brown for *The Armor of Organization*.

T. HARRY WILLIAMS

Contents

List of Illustrations

(Following page 68)

The American Military System:
From the Revolution to 1860

I

IT IS PERHAPS proper at the outset of a series of essays dealing with the history of war to introduce and define a few basic terms. War, like other disciplines, has its own nomenclature or, as some critics of military history would say, its own outlandish jargon. Words that will frequently appear in my presentation are "policy" and "strategy"; there will be little mention of the word "tactics" or little description of that practice of military science which, when depicted in ample detail as it often is in books treating of war, repels the average reader from the study of military history.

Policy is concerned with the purpose for which a war is fought. In democratic governments policy is always determined by the civil government, which decides when, with whom, and for what objective war will be waged and the number of men and the amount of matériel to be allotted to the military branch to achieve the war's purpose. Strategy was originally and narrowly defined as the art of command. As practiced in most American wars of the nineteenth century, it meant that the military took men and supplies made available by the civil branch and planned and executed operations so as to attain the purpose for which war was being fought. Strategy was directed by a general-in-chief if operations were in charge of one man, or by several departmental commanders if, as was often the case, there was no single authoritative head. Tactics is the arrangement and direction of troops in the presence of the enemy when battle is joined.

During the latter half of the nineteenth century strategy began to take on a broader meaning. As both society and war became more technological and complex, strategy became more non-military. It came to include many new elements—economic, psychological, political, scientific—and directors of strategy on the highest level discovered that war was becoming a problem of mobilizing and administering the total resources of a nation. It was a problem that was too vast to be encompassed by any one set of leaders from any one profession, and in particular, it was too vast for professional soldiers, trained as they were in the concept that war was largely a clash between two aggregations of men in uniforms. The psychology of many soldiers was epitomized in the reputed remark of the younger Moltke in 1914 when he was presented with a plan for economic mobilization: "Don't bother me with economics; I am busy conducting the war."

The nature of modern war—its mechanization, its mass armies, its insatiable demands for supplies—dictated a greater civilian participation in the preparation and conduct of war. Perhaps the most important military development of the past century has been the emergence of the civilian as a factor in strategic planning and a force in the military machine. The role of the civilian in modern warfare, although apparent before World War I, was first strikingly illustrated in that titanic struggle which required masses of matériel to satisfy its mass armies. In England, for example, the military men proved incapable of organizing the nation's resources. They seemed unable to envision a war that consumed supplies almost as fast as they were produced, and they failed utterly to devise a procurement program that would provide the armies with weapons and other tools of war. Not until civilians were placed in control of departments charged with procurement functions were the supplies ordered and delivered in the needed amounts. England's experience prompted Winston Churchill to say, "Modern war is total, and it is necessary that technical and professional authorities should be sustained and if necessary directed by heads of government, who have the knowledge which enables them to comprehend not only the military but the political and economic forces at work and who have the power to focus them all upon the goal." [1] Churchill's words are particularly pertinent in our own times, when strategy has become an element of statecraft. Today strategy would have to be very broadly defined: it is the art of utilizing the resources of a nation or, more probably, the resources of a coalition of nations to attain the ends of policy.

One of the great military problems of modern governments has been the question of where to draw a

[1] Edward Mead Earle, Gordon Craig, and Felix Gilbert (eds.), *Makers of Modern Strategy* (Princeton, 1943), 296.

proper and sensible line between the civil and military branches in the function of determining strategy. Or, to put it another way, the problem has been to integrate the thinking of leaders in both branches to the end that an integrated strategy would result. In most of the wars of the ancient, medieval, and early modern periods the issue did not emerge, for in those conflicts the civil and military divisions of government were often, in reality or in effect, in the hands of the same man: Alexander, Julius Caesar, Gustavus Adolphus, Frederick the Great, Napoleon. It was not until the advent of the modern era, about 1800, and coincidental with the rise of representative governments and the triumph of the Industrial Revolution, that the relationship between policy and strategy began to trouble national leaders. Even if the civil governments of the democracies had not been determined to subject the military to control, it was obvious that policy and strategy were inextricably connected and could not be separated into two tidy compartments and determined by two agencies which never consulted each other. It was clear that strategy should be the joint product of the civil and military branches. But what exactly was the strategic function of each branch? How far should civilians, who were amateurs in war, go in imposing their will upon soldiers? How free should soldiers, who were servants of the government, be in deciding strategy?

Over the past century and a half or so of warfare governments, including that of the United States, have sought to provide solutions to these and other questions by establishing within the political framework some arrangement for formalizing and implementing relations between the civil and the military. These arrangements, which are concerned with strategy at the highest level, are the very heart of modern military organizations, and they may be referred to, conveniently and accurately, as command systems. As we survey the development of the American military organization, we shall focus our primary attention on the attempts of the government of the United States to achieve a workable command system. It was not an easy task, and some may doubt that the goal has yet been reached. Once during World War I David Lloyd George tried to express his notions of the proper relationship between civilians and soldiers by saying that what was needed was "trustful cooperation between expert and layman—tendered freely by both, welcomed cordially by both." [2] This was a neat way of putting it, but the reality has never been that neat. Trustful co-operation was not exactly the spirit with which the civil and the military viewed each other on the eve of America's first war, the Revolution.

2

When, in 1775, the Continental Congress named George Washington general-in-chief of its forces, at that moment consisting of the New England

[2] *Ibid.*, 298.

militia (then besieging Boston), which had been designated—and not completely to their liking—as a national army, John Adams instructed his friends in Massachusetts how to receive the commander and his staff. Wishing to honor the Virginian whose appointment he had helped to secure, but remembering the scarcity of supplies, Adams wrote, "I hope the utmost politeness and respect will be shown to these officers on their arrival. The whole army, I think, should be drawn up upon the occasion, and all the pride, pomp, and circumstance of glorious war displayed;—*no powder burned, however.*"

In arranging the nature of Washington's welcome —and the details of a military exercise—the doughty patriot was not ruled solely by considerations of economy. Like other members of the Congress, he had definite ideas about military affairs and definite opinions as to how a war should be run. Obsessed by fears of a military dictatorship, he warned his colleagues to keep "a watchful eye on the army, to see that it does not ravish from them that liberty for which all have been contending"; he believed that he knew as much about war as any soldier, and he was always ready to put generals in their places. He advocated a scheme to have generals elected annually by the Congress, a practice, he claimed, which would keep the officers on their toes and remind them of their subordination to the civil branch.

Quite another matter seemed to excite his cousin Sam Adams, who was interested in the sentiments of soldiers when drinking toasts; if an officer drank to the army before toasting the Congress, Sam wanted to cashier him out of service as a potential Caesar. But no member of the Congress exceeded Dr. Benjamin Rush in certainty of military knowledge and carping attention to military trivia—especially the drinking habits of generals. Rush, who dreaded to hear of a victory by Washington because success for the general would stamp a value on his own qualities of ignorance, negligence, and languor, was convinced that American commanders drank too much. He proposed that the Congress ration intoxicants to the generals and that any officer who consumed more than one quart of whiskey or got drunk more than once in twenty-four hours be reprimanded at the head of his unit. Moreover, he wanted the Congress to require that generals sleep in their boots and that in battle they remain no more than five hundred yards in the rear of their troops.

The officious antics of a few members of the Congress should not obscure the great fact that the Revolution was a serious and important war. It was the first revolutionary war and the first war of ideas of modern times. Because it was a war of ideas, it differed from the usual leisurely, limited-objective conflicts of the eighteenth century. For the Americans, at least, it was a national war, one that went all the way, and sometimes they resorted to rough methods to win it— methods that violated accepted contemporary rules and procedures of warfare, such as embarking on winter campaigns, infiltrating irregular troops behind lines, aiming at individuals in battle, and, a practice which particularly pained the British, shooting at officers, who as gentlemen were supposed to be inviolate from bullets. The Revolution is the longest war in which the United States has engaged, and it was, by the standards of the times and for the rebelling colonies, a stupendous military undertaking.

Out of a total population of two and a half million the Americans furnished 395,858 soldiers, of whom 231,770 served in the Continental Army, the national army raised under the authority of the Continental Congress, and 164,887 in the militia of the states. These figures have to be qualified. They include many duplicates, especially in the militia, and many short-term enlistments in the national service. The Congress, partly because of inexperience and partly because of fear of the military, brought itself with great reluctance to follow Washington's advice to authorize long enlistment periods. The actual number of men serving for any appreciable time was probably 150,000. The largest army ever commanded by Washington numbered 20,000; the average size of his forces fluctuated between 5,000 and 9,000, and at one dark moment he led a band of only 2,000.

It is easy, looking back from the present, to criticize American conduct of the Revolution—to emphasize the reliance upon paper currency, the faulty organization of the services of supply, the sufferings of the army, and the bickering in the higher levels of the government and the army. It is particularly easy to call attention to the shortcomings of the Continental Congress—to highlight its administrative failures and its apparent indecision and timidity. And many of these indictments should be noted, because often the mistakes of the past, when known, will prevent repetition of error in the future. But we should not look so hard for the mistakes that we fail to comprehend the full import of the Revolution itself. After all, the

Americans, with the help of foreign nations it is true, did win their independence. A careful analysis of the Revolution leads one to wonder not that the Americans did so badly but that they did so well—which is the kind of conclusion, I believe, reached by historians after studying most human experiences.

The thirteen colonies, or states, had challenged one of the great powers of the world. They entered into war with a substantial minority of the population opposed to the purposes of the war and another segment lukewarm in its support. They had practically no industry, no army, and no navy. They had almost no government. The Continental Congress, which originally came into being to channel American protests to England, became a government by default; it was in existence when the shooting started, and it was the most available agency to co-ordinate military preparations. Lacking clear or specific powers, it exercised what authority the states would permit or public opinion would support. It organized an army, appointed commanders, sent diplomats to Europe, and financed its military expenses by issuing paper money. If the currency program of the Congress seems ill advised—and it did produce a wild inflation—it should be remembered that the Congress lacked the power to tax and that in a poor country like America paper money was the only financial recourse. Moreover, by decreeing that its currency must be accepted at face value, the Congress performed an act of truly revolutionary vigor. When its record is examined, most of its failures—in providing supplies for the armies, in handling disbursements of money, in mobilizing economic resources—will be found to be of an administrative nature. And this is not surprising when one considers that the Congress had no established civil service, no going bureaus and departments to administer its business. There was no separate executive, which meant that the Congress, a plural body, had to implement its own measures. In the situation in which it had to operate, it did a remarkably good job in supervising the conduct of the war.

The policy of the American government, that is, of the Continental Congress representing the states, was to achieve independence. The strategy employed to accomplish their purpose was largely forced upon the Americans by the nature of British strategy. Commanding the sea and based conveniently in adjacent Canada, the British struck at key points on the coast, from which they could advance into the interior, and invaded northern New York with a view to splitting the colonies into two parts. American strategy was designed to defend places about to be attacked or to defeat British armies attempting to move inland from prepared bases. In brief, on the highest strategic level the Americans had to fight defensively, but on a lower level they were not precluded from an offensive strategy, that is, from attacking individual British armies.

The machinery, or the organization, to regulate relations between the civil and the military was fairly sound in theory and as good as conditions permitted. The Congress, as the supreme civil authority, asserted its power to raise the armed forces and draw up regulations for their governance, to appoint all officers of general grade (the states insisted on appointing line officers in the Continental Army through the rank of colonel), and to make promotions. In general, these were proper exercises of civil power, although the Congress would have been better advised to leave the matter of promotions to Washington and other commanders, that is, to have the generals recommend and the Congress merely confirm or deny promotions.

The resolution of the Continental Congress naming Washington commander-in-chief in 1775 and the commission issued to him invested the general with broad powers to command, under that body, the American land forces; the language is plain that Washington was expected to direct the strategic operations of all American armies. Language alone, however, could not establish a satisfactory command system. Nothing in the resolution or the commission dealt with the formulation of strategy. Just who, for example, was supposed to initiate a strategic plan, Washington or the Congress? Should either be required to secure the approval of the other before putting a plan into operation? And if consultation between the two was desirable, how would a body like the Congress make known its ideas to Washington? The whole hard problem was complicated by the fact that Washington, in addition to being supervisor of all armies, was also the commander of a field army, a post which alone is usually important enough to occupy fully the energies of one man. Washington was in direct command of the Middle Department (lower New York, New Jersey, Pennsylvania, Delaware, Maryland); the two other principal departments, the Northern and the Southern, had their own commanders who were subject, at least in theory, to Washington's directions.

At first the Congress attempted to exercise strategic function itself; that is, the delegates as a unit tried to devise strategy. That body ordered an invasion of Canada in 1775, which was a sound enough idea although the preparations to support the expedition were inadequate, and directed that New York City be defended in 1776, which was not a very sound idea although Washington had originally had the same thought.

Being a plural agency and busy with affairs of state, the Congress, however, soon realized that it could not actively direct the war. Accordingly, it created in 1776 an agency composed of five of its own members —the Board of War—to represent it in dealing with the military. In 1777, after the loss of Philadelphia and ensuing criticism of the Congress, the composition of the board was changed. It was now to consist of three persons not members of the Congress and was to include, on Washington's advice, military men. Still another alteration was made in 1778; the personnel of the board was fixed at five, two members of the Congress and three non-members.

The Board of War, then, was the executive arm of the Congress in the area of strategy and in the entire field of military affairs. The command system consisted of a committee representing the civil authority and a general-in-chief. Although far from perfect, it was as sensible and simple a system as could have been devised in the kind of government the Americans then had. Certainly a board which included soldiers should have been able to co-operate with reasonable efficiency with the soldier who headed the armies. And the arrangement did, in fact, work better than one might suppose from reading some of the histories of the Revolution or some of the anguished comments in Washington's letters. When it did not work—and there were many occasions when it fell short—the failure was due to the human elements in the system, particularly to the very human faults of certain members of the Congress. At once we are reminded that the efficiency of any agency of government depends as much on the nature of the men at the top as on symmetry of organization.

The most deplorable qualities displayed by the Congress, or by some of its members, in dealing with Washington are usually ascribed to that body's fear of a military tyranny and to its desire to put the military in its place. Although these motives were undoubtedly present, the impression is inescapable that the worst mistakes of the Congress were the result of sheer ignorance of war and the inability of a new and untried government to achieve efficient administration in any area, military or otherwise. Frequently, the Congress sent orders directly to the commander of the Northern Department; in 1780 it removed the Southern theater from Washington's control, only to restore it when the delegates' hand-picked commander, Horatio Gates, suffered an ignominious defeat. In these and other similar situations the Congress was well within its proper command powers, but good administration would have dictated that Washington be at least consulted in each case.

When the Board of War was reconstructed with military members, a step which Washington had recommended, known enemies of the general were appointed to the agency in a clumsy attempt to assert

15

civil supremacy. But the most serious indictment of the Congress is that it did not too much but too little. Too many times it simply dawdled. One of the most frequent complaints in Washington's letters is that he could not get the Congress to answer his communications. He waited three months for the legislators to authorize him to increase his artillery forces before acting on his own initiative. Once when he went to Philadelphia to seek a personal audience with the Congress, he was kept waiting for days. The Congress even delayed to inform the general-in-chief of the French alliance, although the prospect of foreign aid was a vital factor in strategic planning. It is no wonder that Washington wailed that prompt decisions, even though against him, would have been less damaging than procrastination.

No civil power ever had less to fear from a general than did the Congress from Washington. He was the very model of the proper citizen-soldier. Douglas S. Freeman, in his biography of Washington, lists the rules that guided the general in his relations with the Congress: always to acknowledge the supremacy of the civil branch and the subordination of the military, to refrain from public criticism of the Congress, and to keep that body, or at least discreet members of it, fully informed at all times of his plans and operations.[3] It is partly because he was so perceptive about the role of the soldier in a democracy that Washington stands as the supreme figure of the Revolution.

---

[3] Douglas S. Freeman, *George Washington* (7 vols., New York, 1948–54), V, 487–88.

3

We may pass briefly over the American military experience during the Articles of Confederation period. Perhaps the most significant military event of those experimental years was the plan Washington proposed to the Congress for the organization of the land forces—a plan which, in the general's opinion, would provide the United States with an army strong enough to repel any attack. At the end of the Revolution the Congress asked Washington to recommend a military policy for the new nation. After consulting with various of his generals, Washington wrote a treatise which he entitled *Sentiments on a Peace Establishment*. In this remarkable document, which suffers by summary, he advised that the country's first line of defense be a small but proficient regular army; supplementing the professionals would be a large citizen army composed of the militia of the several states, which would be placed under national supervision and trained by officers educated at a national military academy. Congress received Washington's report and filed it safely away.

In 1784, when the forces of the Revolution were disbanded, the Congress retained eighty men in military service, caretakers to watch over supplies. As Indian troubles threatened in the West or domestic insurrection flamed in the East (Shays's Rebellion), the Congress called on the states for militia or attempted to enlist volunteers in a national force. When the new government of the Constitution took over in 1789 it found an "army" of 595 men, commanded by

17

Lieutenant Colonel Josiah Harmar, and a military administration, presided over by "Secretary at War" Henry Knox and consisting of three clerks and a messenger. The contingent expenses of Knox's department reached the staggering total of $176 a year.

Military developments between 1789 and the outbreak of the next war in 1812 may also be presented in summary form. For convenient classification we may divide the events of those years as falling in the Federalist or the Republican administrations. In the Federalist period the land forces consisted, very much as in the Confederation era, of a small and not particularly efficient regular army raised by voluntary enlistment and of the militia of the states, whose organizations seemed to become more social and political and less military by the year. The size of the regular army varied, being originally fixed at 1,216 and then expanded as Indian wars in the Northwest Territory and the threat of conflict with France showed the need for a larger force. By the end of the century the army numbered approximately 5,400 men.

Conditions of army life were not such as to attract men who could make a living doing anything else. For private soldiers the pay was three dollars a month; the yearly clothing allowance was one hat, one coat, one vest, two woolen overalls, two linen overalls, four pairs of shoes, four shirts, two pairs of socks, and one blanket; the food consisted largely of meat, flour, and whiskey, no vegetables being regularly issued until after 1815.

President Washington made a notable attempt to induce Congress to adopt his plan to place the militia under national supervision but could not overcome the opposition of civilians, who were fearful of increasing the military establishment, and of the militia, who did not want to become efficient. The Militia Bill of 1792 did require all able-bodied males between eighteen and forty-five to be enrolled in the militia of their states, but with Washington's idea of federal inspection amended out, the measure was almost meaningless. As most states did not enforce the compulsory service feature or require serious training procedures, the militia steadily deteriorated. On the muster rolls of this phantom citizen army were 674,000 men, a larger force than the Coalition brought against Napoleon.

In the field of administration the best that can be said for the Federalists is that they achieved a simple pattern of central direction for a small establishment. The Secretary of War and the Secretary of the Navy (the latter department was created in 1798), acting as the civil deputies of the President, ran their departments with relatively little interference from above. The three men who headed the War office between 1789 and 1800—Knox, Timothy Pickering, and James McHenry—were only mediocre administrators, and their organization was not able to cope with large or sudden emergencies. Its limitations were cruelly revealed in the major military undertakings of the Federalist period—the Harmar, St. Clair, and Wayne expeditions against the Indians, which were marked by glaring and wretched deficiencies in the mobilization process and in the supply services.

In the army's organizational setup the office of general-in-chief was not clearly delineated or recognized. The practice was to acknowledge as command-

19

ing general the officer of highest grade or, if several held the same grade, the one with the senior commission. Brigadier General Josiah Harmar (1790–91), Major General Arthur St. Clair (1791–92), and Major General Anthony Wayne (1792–96), the first three commanding generals, held the position because they were appointed to lead forces, the only forces possessed by the government at the moment, against the Northwestern Indians. After the defeat of the Indians, Congress abolished the rank of major general, and Brigadier General James Wilkinson became the ranking officer. He maintained this position— except for the interlude of the French war scare (1798–1800) when Washington became lieutenant general and was followed by Alexander Hamilton as major general—until 1812, when the grade of major general was revived. Indeed, in the first eight years of the Jeffersonian Republican era Wilkinson was the only officer of general grade in the army.

The attitudes of the Republicans toward military matters were part of their ideology or official program. They feared the presence of a standing army, and they were determined to cut governmental expenses to a minimum—and what better place to start cutting than the military establishment, which in happy and secure America could be restricted to functioning as a frontier constabulary force? Secretary of the Treasury Gallatin voiced the psychology of the Jeffersonians when he wrote, "The distribution of our little army to distant garrisons where hardly any other inhabitant is to be found is the most eligible arrangement of that perhaps necessary evil that can be contrived. But I never want to see the face of one in our cities and intermixed with the people."

In accordance with their philosophy the Republicans fixed the size of the army at 3,350. The War Department consisted of the Secretary and a dozen clerks. But worse than the lack of adequate personnel in the War office, from the military viewpoint, was the absence of sound concepts of administration. Whatever virtues the Jeffersonians possessed in other areas of government, administration was not their forte. Henry Dearborn, who was Secretary from 1801 to 1809, was a genial man who had served with distinction in the Revolution, but he made little impress on the civil and military organization under his control. His successor, William Eustis, has been described by J. R. Jacobs as "a military tinker" with "a second-rate mind" and "a piddling incompetent." In discussing the organization of the War Department under these secretaries Leonard D. White writes in his monumental administrative history of the United States, "The system . . . lacked integration, responsibility, unity, and energy, and was utterly inadequate for even the most modest operations. There were no central agencies of the War Department for procurement, for record keeping or for control, other than the accountant and the clerks who copied figures and letters." [4] These defects were imbedded deeply in the military system; they could not be easily or quickly eradicated in the stress of war.

[4] James Ripley Jacobs, *The Beginning of the U.S. Army, 1783–1812* (Princeton, 1947), 363, 383; Leonard D. White, *The Jeffersonians* (New York, 1951), 215.

4

The War of 1812 occupies an unhappy place in our history books. Undertaken without preparation, conducted without knowledge, and fought without skill—this is the usual description of it—it seems to have been a war that provided no military lesson, that accomplished nothing, and that is better forgotten. Actually, however, it was not nearly so bad. Although in the first two years of the war American armies suffered some of the most humiliating disasters in our history, in the last year, demonstrating tremendous improvement, they defeated the best the British had to offer. The navy, although not large enough to be a major factor in ocean warfare, proved consistently that ship for ship it was superior to the navy that ruled the seas, and on the inland lakes it swung the military balance definitely in favor of the Americans. If most of the war's lessons are negative, showing what should not be done, and if its conduct exhibits the dangers of prosecuting a war with weak administrators and a faulty administrative system, it should be noted that some of the lessons were learned and that attempts were made to improve the system—too late to affect the course of the war but carrying promise for the future. Finally, if the test of a successful war is that the position of the nation is stronger afterward than before, the War of 1812 was a valid, though not a victorious, war. Contrary to the opinions of many congressmen and commentators, the Korean conflict was not the first war that we did not, technically, win.

One of the most curious features of the war was the failure of the central government to mobilize effectively the nation's resources. Although the government was more securely established and more powerful than the Continental Congress, it did no better and sometimes did worse than its counterpart during the Revolution. Again we are reminded that often men are more important than systems. In sporadic preparations that immediately preceded the war, Congress had authorized increasing the army to 35,000. Two weeks before war was declared, the Senate asked the Secretary of War to state the number of troops in service and their readiness for combat. The Secretary passed the request on to the inspector general, who reported that he did not know the strength of the army because almost no recent returns had been received and that he could not evaluate its condition because he had not inspected it!

Probably 6,744 men comprised the army in 1812. As the war progressed, Congress passed legislation to enlarge the army, providing for both short- and long-term enlistments. Both Congress and the President, however, preferred to rely primarily on the unreliable state militia instead of on a national army. The number of men enlisted in national service was as follows: regular army, 56,032; volunteers, 10,110; rangers, 3,049. The bulk of the armed forces was furnished by the militia, of whom 458,463 (including duplicates) were called into the field. Because the service terms of the militia were limited by law, the great majority of the troops served for periods of less than six months. This mobilization performance may be contrasted with that of the harassed Continental Congress, which succeeded in enlisting some 231,000 regulars and employed only 164,000 militia soldiers.

Over the forces thus raised there presided in the first two years of the war one of the choicest collections of incompetent generals in our military history. Those holding the highest grade were elderly officers who had served in the Revolution, often with distinction but in minor positions where they had no opportunity to command troops in large numbers. Henry Dearborn, the senior major general, who had directed a regiment in the Revolution, was sixty-one years of age; the other major general, Thomas Pinckney, who had been a guerrilla leader in the Revolution, was sixty-three. Among the brigadiers, William Hull, who would lead an army to disaster at Detroit, was sixty; the senior brigadier, Wilkinson, at fifty-five, was a comparative youth. The other brigadier generals had come into the army since the Revolution and had not only never commanded sizable bodies of troops but had never seen any substantial number of men under arms. The capacities of all the generals from Dearborn down were strained by the requirements of commanding even the modest field armies employed in the war, armies which varied from 3,000 to 7,000 men. By the end of 1813, after a series of defeats and debacles, nearly all of the original generals had been forced out of service or relieved of duty, and into their places had stepped younger and abler officers who had fought their way up to eminence, men like Jacob Brown, Winfield Scott, and Alexander Macomb. Although all of the first generals and most of those later attaining the grade had had some kind of military experience prior to the war—in the Revolution, in the

24

Indian conflicts, or in the militia—only one, George Izard, who had been educated abroad, had received formal military training. The Military Academy at West Point had been established in 1802, and by the close of the war had turned out 120 graduates, the majority of whom saw service in the war but, being junior officers, in the lower echelons of command.

The confusion and incompetence that characterized the highest level of command throughout the war is amply illustrated in the preliminaries of the British occupation of Washington in 1814. One unhappy episode reveals, as does perhaps no other event in the conflict, the utter inability of the men in charge of the government and the military system to realize their proper functions and to think intelligently about war. A regiment of Virginia militia appeared in the capital on the eve of the battle for its defense and asked for guns and other equipment. Their commander first went to President Madison, who directed him to the Secretary of War, who told him to report to the officer in charge of military stores. This official, however, was away at his country home. Finally, the Virginians prevailed on a subordinate to issue them guns. Instead of tossing the guns to the soldiers, this perfect bureaucrat counted them out, one by one— the enemy was approaching the city at the time —and then, to make sure that the taxpayers' supplies were not being wasted, insisted on counting them over again! It is perhaps unnecessary to remark that the regiment never got into the fighting.

To command the forces being hastily assembled to defend the capital, President Madison, over the objections of the Secretary of War, appointed William H.

Winder. The Secretary then took the position that the President was directing the defense of the city and refused to shoulder any further responsibility. Winder was an incredibly incompetent general. Of him Henry Adams wrote, dipping his pen in acid, "When he might have prepared defences, he acted as scout; when he might have fought, he still scouted; when he retreated, he retreated in the wrong direction; when he fought, he thought only of retreat; and whether scouting, retreating, or fighting, he never betrayed an idea." [5] As the British approached Washington, Madison, accompanied by several cabinet members, rode out to be with the troops. For two days and for reasons that have never been discovered, he followed Winder in his aimless scouting trips around the countryside. He was present on the field at the beginning of the battle of Bladensburg and nearly rode into the British lines before retiring to Washington to arrange for an evacuation in case of disaster. Although he had told the cabinet to meet him at Frederick, Maryland, he left the city in another direction and started to follow Winder again.

Also participating in the campaign was Secretary of State Monroe, who undertook a scouting expedition of two days and then appeared at Bladensburg, where he altered the disposition of some troops without their commander's knowledge. Henry Adams remarked sourly that Monroe's services were not very valuable, either as a scout or as a general.[6] None of the

[5] Henry Adams, *History of the United States . . . during the Administrations of Thomas Jefferson and James Madison* (9 vols., New York, 1889–91), VIII, 153.

[6] *Ibid.*, 151.

chief actors in these fantastic scenes seemed to have understood their proper roles. In the words of Leonard White, "All were irresistibly drawn to the field of battle, where none of them should have been. No one of them performed correctly the function which his office imposed upon him." [7]

The primary objective of American policy in the War of 1812 was to acquire Canada. American strategy, therefore, had to be offensive; to attain the coveted territory armies would have to invade it and occupy key areas. With Britain fighting a war in Europe which absorbed the bulk of her army, the seizure of Canada was thought to be an easy mission —which it would have been for even a reasonably efficient invader. By 1814, however, the British, having disposed of Napoleon, were able for the first time to commit substantial forces to the American war and go over to the offensive. Then the Americans were forced to resort to a defensive strategy, very similar to the type they had employed in the Revolution.

In the first year of the war the function of formulating strategy was loosely performed by Madison, his cabinet, and General Dearborn. Although Dearborn was the senior general, he was not a general-in-chief but a departmental commander. No officer during the war held a position similar to Washington's in the Revolution. Nevertheless, Dearborn advised the President and the Cabinet on grand strategy, and he seems to have been largely responsible for the triple invasion of Canada in 1812 which ruined so many reputations and cast a shadow on his own. After the terrible fiascoes of that year Secretary of War Eustis

[7] White, *Jeffersonians*, 222–23.

27

resigned, and to his place the President named John Armstrong, one of the few forceful men to hold office in the Madison administration. Armstrong immediately made himself the dominating figure in the command system.

Few cabinet members have assumed office under such trying circumstances. Selected by Madison only after others had rejected the job, Armstrong was barely confirmed by the Senate. At all times he lacked the confidence of Madison and his cabinet associates, who feared his known presidential ambitions and resented his harsh and open criticism of Virginia's influence in the government. Although he had served in the Revolution, he was a civilian, not a soldier, and a politician by profession. The first Secretary to hold his office during an actual war, he was also, through a strange mixture of energy and indolence, the first strong Secretary. It was largely owing to his efforts that the old Revolutionary generals were laid on the shelf and new men installed in the important commands. But, although Armstrong was right in sweeping out the ancients, his judgment as to whom to put in their places was not always sound. He got rid of Dearborn on the country's Northern border, but to succeed him in command of one of the most important expeditions of the war he appointed Wilkinson. In the words of Colonel William A. Ganoe, "Age and infirmity gave place to age and fatuity." [8]

Armstrong's most remarkable accomplishment was to make of his office something it had never been before and has never been since, and something which

[8] William A. Ganoe, *History of the United States Army* (New York, 1924), 132.

in an efficient military organization it should not be. Serving under a complaisant executive and in an un-co-ordinated military system, this vigorous man, who was the President's civil deputy, became also, for a period, a kind of combined chief of staff and general-in-chief. He framed strategy and directed its execution, sometimes going to the theaters of operation to oversee the carrying-out of his plans. Indeed, he wanted to establish his headquarters permanently in northern New York, where he could command the invasion of Canada without presidential interference. Madison forbade this move, but in 1813 Armstrong took the War Department to Sackets Harbor on Lake Ontario for two months to supervise the un-successful offensives of Wilkinson and General Wade Hampton.

In 1814, the last year of the war, Armstrong's power waned. Madison, urged on by Monroe, began to pull the reins on his ambitious Secretary. Armstrong was instructed not to issue orders to departmental commanders without securing Madison's approval and was required to submit his strategic plans to the President and the cabinet for consideration. We find Armstrong saying disgustedly that the adoption of one of his schemes had been delayed by "a discrepancy in the opinions of the Cabinet." After the fall of Washington he was allowed to resign, and he disappeared from the military scene. But while he was present, he left his mark. Although he did not understand his proper function, he infused into the conduct of the war an energy and a decisiveness that no other official could have provided.

Impressed by the disasters of the war and the inadequacies of the military system, the Congress acted during the war and again soon after its close to improve the organization of the army and the navy. Legislation passed in 1813 created for the army an agency that was called the General Staff. Here, at its first appearance, we must be careful to avoid a confusion of terms. The staff we are discussing was not a general staff in the modern meaning of the term. It was not a collective body, and it was not concerned with strategy and co-ordination. Rather, it was a group of officers that came to be housed in Washington, each one of whom was charged with an administrative or housekeeping function under the direction of the Secretary of War.

As originally defined, the General Staff was comprised of the adjutant general, the inspector general, the quartermaster general, the commissary general of ordnance, the paymaster, and the assistant topographical engineer. Each member performed his own duties, and, reporting to the Secretary, went pretty much his own way. With the officers attached to the staff settled in Washington near the Secretary, a significant new pattern of organization emerged. These men became the professional advisers of the Secretary, and as they enlarged their functions, they increased their personnel, bringing to the capital other officers who were specialists like themselves. Soon they headed staff groups, and the development of the bureau system within the War Department was under way. For the first time in its history the War Department contained acknowledged experts who were responsible for executing specialized functions; for the first time it was possible for the Secretary to delegate authority to responsible professional associates. No longer was the department a simple, unco-ordinated agency consisting of a civilian head and a few clerks. With little change the General Staff organization would endure until 1903.

Two years after the creation of the General Staff, Congress authorized a somewhat similar body for the navy, the Board of Navy Commissioners. This three-man agency, to be composed of officers not below the rank of post captain, was charged with the function of advising the Secretary of the Navy on matters of naval establishment and particularly on the construction and equipment of vessels. Unlike the General Staff, however, it was to operate only as a group, and its work was entirely advisory. Although it rendered valuable service to the civilian head, it was abolished in 1842 largely because its decisions were being delayed by disagreements. Congress then assigned the board's duties to five bureaus which resembled the agencies in the General Staff.

5

The long interlude of peace between the close of the second war with England and the outbreak of war with Mexico in 1846 witnessed a number of important developments in the military system. Their broad effect was to make the military establishment

31

larger and more efficient than in any previous period. The size of the regular army, although still small, was fixed at a higher peacetime figure than ever before in our history, varying from 6,000 to 8,000 to 10,000 to 12,000. For the first time since the Revolution the position of commanding general was clearly established and recognized. In 1821 Congress stipulated that only one officer should possess the grade of major general and indicated that the holder of this rank should act as military director of the land forces. Before the Civil War the generals-in-chief of the army were Jacob Brown (1821–28), Alexander Macomb (1828–41), and Winfield Scott (1841–61).

These three men were extremely competent soldiers, and one of them, Scott, would demonstrate in the Mexican War that he deserved to be ranked in the select group of great American battle captains. Their continued presence in the army illustrated a significant development in the military system and in American social values: the material rewards and prestige status of a military career were becoming sufficient to attract and hold able individuals. The army could feel that it was doing something important in the national scheme, and officers, at least those in the higher grades, could believe that they were people whose worth was recognized by other social groups. The day when the military establishment was tolerated as a necessary evil was passing. Not that there was anything glamorous about the army's work. The regular forces, stationed at a hundred posts all over the country, built forts and seacoast fortifications, constructed military roads, ran surveys and conducted explorations in the West, and policed and fought

Indians. Although such duties were often dull and seemed, especially to young officers just out of West Point and bursting with big ideas, to be completely without value, the army was, as more discerning officers realized, playing a necessary and important role in the expansion of the nation.

One big reason for the higher level of officer competence was the improved facilities for military education. West Point, under the leadership of Sylvanus Thayer who became superintendent in 1817, developed into a first-rate officer-training school. Although it retained its original emphasis on engineering and stressed tactics to the neglect of strategy, it turned out graduates who were thoroughly versed in the technical aspects of war. By 1846 the Academy had graduated approximately 1,000 students, of whom about one half stayed in the army. The others, after performing their required hitch of service, resigned their commissions, because they either despaired of promotion or were seduced by the promise of more lucrative positions in civil life. Nevertheless, West Point amply proved its worth in the Mexican War; for the first time in our military history American armies contained large numbers of officers who had had a formal military education. Although the West Pointers, as in the War of 1812, functioned in the lower echelons of command, they contributed mightily to the American victory in 1846. The Naval Academy, established in 1845, would not make its influence felt until the Civil War.

The army also manifested a strong desire for self-education. At the instigation of interested officers and with the encouragement of the War Department,

33

two service schools—they might be termed graduate schools—were set up: the artillery school of instruction at Fort Monroe, Virginia (1824), and the infantry school of practice at Jefferson Barracks, St. Louis (1827). A number of officers published manuals dealing with tactics and the training of soldiers; one of the authors was General Scott. Even a few books on strategy—the higher art of war—came from the pens of American officers, the most notable of which were Henry W. Halleck's *Elements of Military Art and Science* (1846) and Dennis H. Mahan's *Advanced-Guard, Outpost . . . Service, with the Essential Principles of Strategy* (1847). All in all, the army was coming of age.

But from the organizational point of view, the most significant developments of these years occurred in the War Department itself, which from 1817 to 1825 was guided by the strong hands of the first great Secretary of War, John C. Calhoun. Of Calhoun's administration of the War office his biographer writes, without exaggeration: "The organization of the War Department was given a form so nearly definitive that no essential changes were needed, even to cope with the shock of Civil War forty years later, and it long served as the model after which other departments were patterned." [9] Among his accomplishments, Calhoun completed the establishment of the general staff system in Washington, asserted civilian control over the military through the medium of the commanding general, chose able staff officers to whom he delegated authority, and in general improved the

[9] Charles M. Wiltse, *John C. Calhoun, Nationalist, 1782–1828* (Indianapolis, 1944), 297.

efficiency and morale of the entire army. Not the least of his services was the series of brilliant reports in which he described his work to Congress. Although addressed to the legislators, they were also directed at the people and were in reality treatises on military policy and the place of the military in a republic. In their grasp of fundamental principles and in their educational content they deserve to be ranked with Alexander Hamilton's reports on economics and finance.

6

Only in recent years has the Mexican War come to occupy a respectable place in the national historical consciousness. Once denounced in the textbooks as a wicked war of aggression against a weaker neighbor, it is now recognized that the United States had some justification for resorting to war and that the acquisition of the territory seized from Mexico was an inevitable phase in the process of American history, a result that might have been delayed but could not have been prevented. Coincidentally, President Polk, who used to be pictured as the scheming villain of the piece, is now acknowledged to have been a strong executive, a leader with vision, and one of the great American empire-builders. In such ways do historical perspectives—and reputations—shift from one gen-

35

eration to another. Undoubtedly, the present tendency to seek out affirmative values in the national past is responsible for the more favorable view of the war which gained for this country the princely domain of the Southwest and California.

In the struggle with Mexico, American operations were, for the first time in our military history, conducted with relative efficiency. Troops were raised and transported over long distances to the theaters of war in Mexico, and armies were moved into a country as large as twenty Ohios and kept supplied while they were there. An example of American competence is afforded by Scott's campaign against Mexico City. After his forces were landed at Vera Cruz, in what, incidentally, was the first major joint amphibious operation of the United States army and navy, and after the city was secured as a base, Scott began a march of 260 miles to the enemy capital. He completed the movement without a reverse in six months with an army that usually numbered 10,000, half of whom were untrained volunteers. In 1861–63 it would take 30,000 French regulars eighteen months to reach the same objective against a less powerful Mexican army, and en route they suffered a bad defeat at Puebla.

Factors that help to explain the improved proficiency of American arms over the performances in earlier wars were the rapidly expanding national economy, which was able to produce much of the matériel of war without undue strain; the existence of the General Staff, which made its influence felt in many areas but particularly in the organization of the services of supply; the control of the sea lanes by the navy, which enabled the Americans to land forces on the Mexican coast and to utilize water lines of communication; and the presence in the army, at all levels of command, of a number of reasonably competent officers.

Only in the mobilization process did the men who were running the war display the fumbling ineptitude that had marked the conduct of earlier wars. Following the advice of Polk, who expected a short war, Congress, instead of filling up the regular army, decided to rely on a force of national volunteers. These men were allowed to enlist for twelve months *or* for the duration of the war. At the same time, enlistees in the regular army were required to sign up for five years or the duration. Naturally, most of those who wanted to fight Mexicans chose the volunteers. A total of 104,000 troops was raised, of whom 60,000 were volunteers; 32,000, regulars; and 12,000, militia. Thus, as in the Revolution and the War of 1812, a majority of the men under arms served for short periods—for periods so brief as to often hinder military operations. In Scott's march on Mexico City, for example, the commanding general had to halt his army for months midway to his objective in order to discharge several twelve-month units and await reinforcements. Despite the large number of troops raised, American field armies were always small in size. At various times Scott and Zachary Taylor each commanded forces of over 14,000, of whom probably 10,000 were available for battle. In most of the encounters of the war the Americans were outnumbered.

The quality of high-ranking officers may be rated as

competent, but, with the exception of Scott, no better. Even simple competence, however, had not been consistently present in the two previous wars. The generals who directed armies were Scott, Taylor, John E. Wool, and Stephen Kearny. Scott was a fine soldier; Taylor, while he had his faults, was aggressive and knew how to direct his men; Wool and Kearny were sound routine officers. Prominent among the division and brigade commanders were William J. Worth, David E. Twiggs, Robert Patterson, Gideon Pillow, John A. Quitman, P. F. Smith, George Cadwalader, Franklin Pierce, and James Shields; almost without exception they did creditable jobs. It is interesting and important to note that, while the four army commanders had been professional soldiers before the war, only two of the subordinate generals, Worth and Twiggs, had been associated with the army. The others came into the war from civilian life, where a few had had militia experience; they were amateurs leading a largely amateur army. Not one of the generals, even the professionals, had received a formal military education. All the education was concentrated at the lower command levels, among the West Pointers, who as junior officers experienced their first taste of actual war and made their first important contribution to an American war effort. That the contribution, especially that of the engineers, was substantial was universally acknowledged. Scott himself testified that the Academy's products were a major factor in the American victory.

James K. Polk was the second President to hold office during a war and the first actually to function as commander-in-chief. Madison had acted as a wartime President, but he had not exercised his powers as a director of war. Polk, who must be ranked as one of our strong chief executives, exercised his authority to the hilt. He determined the general strategy of the war; he forced the War and Navy and other departments to submit their financial estimates to him for review, thus becoming the first President to operate as chief budget officer of the government, and he supervised in detail the work of the General Staff. As Leonard White has emphasized, Polk "proved that a President could run a war." [10]

It is no exaggeration to say that the command system consisted of President Polk—with General-in-Chief Scott and the cabinet acting, when the chief executive called on them, as consultants and advisers. When the war started, Scott had no general plan of strategy prepared, and he immediately proceeded to embroil himself in a personal and political quarrel with the administration. Polk, labeling the general "scientific and visionary" and regarding him as a Whig aspirant for the presidency, kept him in Washington doing nothing important until the later stages of the war, then sent him to Mexico. Thus the chief role of the commanding general in the war was to act as a field commander. Polk used the cabinet as a sounding board to test his own views and as a co-ordinating agency to unify the military, political, and foreign aspects of the war. Every important segment of the conflict—strategic plans, instructions to diplomats, blockade rules, choice of generals—was placed before the cabinet for discussion and decision. If some of these items seem strange matters for the

[10] Leonard D. White, *The Jacksonians* (New York, 1954), 50.

39

President's civil advisers to be considering, it is to be remembered that the cabinet was the only body then existing that could co-ordinate the various war functions; such a task would have been beyond the capacities of the General Staff. In addition to utilizing the services of the full cabinet, Polk supervised directly the routine work of the heads of the War and Navy departments and co-ordinated their activities. For the first time, departments other than State were brought directly under executive control.

President Polk's diary, almost startling in its frankness, reveals how the author determined the broad outlines of strategy. As the policy of the United States was to force Mexico to agree to a peace which would cede territory this country had previously offered to purchase, American strategy had to be offensive in nature. Polk's plan was simple and essentially sound: invade and occupy the northern provinces of Mexico and California, thus compelling Mexico to conclude peace on American terms. Immediately after war had been declared, he informed Secretary of War William L. Marcy and General Scott of his design. "I had a long conference with them concerning the plan of conducting the war with Mexico," he wrote in his diary. "I gave it as my opinion that the first movement should be to march a competent force into the northern provinces and seize and hold them until peace was made. In this they concurred." Two days after this meeting he discussed the strategy of the war with the cabinet: "The plan of the campaign against Mexico was considered and particularly against the northern provinces. I presented my views to the Cabinet and they were approved." When Polk's plan failed to bring Mexico to concede defeat, he decided on another—an invasion of Mexico from Vera Cruz, designed to capture Mexico City. At the same time Scott proposed a similar movement, and it was this operation, prepared and executed by Scott, that finally ended the war.

The President, then, either framed the major strategy of the war or participated in its formulation. In addition, he interested himself in and attempted to supervise the administration of all areas of the military system. Determined to infuse energy into every aspect of the war, he constantly watched the General Staff agencies, especially those concerned with supplies, and prodded them to perform their functions. On one occasion he went so far as to suggest to the quartermaster general that the army ought to dispense with baggage wagons and use mules instead. But on this issue not even Polk could overcome military conservatism. Leonard White summarizes Polk's various activities by saying, "It had been demonstrated that a civilian commander in chief could—and did—function effectively as the single center for direction, authorization, coordination, and in lesser degree for control of a larger military and naval effort. All lines concentrated in the White House . . . Thus was achieved a genuine unity of command . . . that succeeded in keeping in coordination the various movements in the field." [11]

[11] *Ibid.,* 65.

7

The military organization had worked well in the Mexican War, but it had also revealed faults and shortcomings that became more marked after the war and that promised to handicap it seriously in a larger conflict. Basically, the trouble resided in the ambiguous relations between the Secretary of War, the bureau heads of the General Staff, and the commanding general. In the civilian area of the War office the organization hardly differed from that of Washington's time; there were more employees, but they were still clerks. With no administrative assistants the Secretary, unless he was an unusually strong character, found it difficult to control the army machine. The bureau heads were officers who had reached their positions by seniority and who believed that they had a vested tenure of service. Knowing that nothing but a court-martial or an earthquake could shake them out of their jobs, they tended to follow an independent course and avoid supervision. When the General Staff was created in 1813, there was no commanding general, and the members reported to the Secretary. After 1821, when the office of General-in-Chief was recognized, the staff heads were in theory made responsible to the commanding general. Actually, they regarded themselves his equal and sought to deny his authority. As between the Secretary and the general, they leaned to the former but preferred neither. Complicating the whole arrangement was the hazy relation of the General-in-Chief to the Secretary. Obviously the general was the Secretary's military deputy, but the extent of the Secretary's authority over the military organization had never been exactly defined. Generally, the Secretary tried to exert direct control over the "staff" segment of the army, and the general fought to keep both staff and "line" under his direction.

When this organization was in the hands of disputatious men, it could be almost wrecked by personal feuds. Such a pass was reached in the Pierce administration when Jefferson Davis was Secretary of War and Scott was commanding general. Both were noted epistolary brawlers, and they engaged in a series of unseemly quarrels. In their exchange of letters they hurled such phrases as "peevish temper," "arrogance and superciliousness," and "monstrous calumnies." Finally Davis wrote Scott, "Your petulance, characteristic egotism and recklessness of accusation have imposed on me the task of unveiling some of your deformities," which turned out to be "querulousness, insubordination, greed of lucre and want of truth." Nothing daunted by this barrage, Scott replied, "My silence, under the new provocation, has been the result, first, of pity, and next, forgetfulness. Compassion is always due to an enraged imbecile, who lays about him in blows which hurt only himself, or who, at the worst, seeks to stifle his opponent by dint of naughty words." These angry insults were ominous harbingers of a command relationship that would trouble the military system in the far future. They were also equally ominous precursors of the immediate future —of the Civil War when the two men would be command antagonists.

☆ ☆ ☆ ☆ ☆ ☆ ☆ ☆ ☆ ☆ ☆

*The Military Systems of
North and South*

I

TRITE IT MAY BE to say that the Civil War was the first of the modern wars, but this is a truth that needs to be repeated. If the Civil War was not quite total, it missed totality by only a narrow margin. Instead of ending a military cycle as historians once thought, the war began a new one that has not yet been completed. In two ways the Civil War differed from previous conflicts of the modern era in both America and Europe. First, as a war of ideas on the part of both participants, it was a struggle of unlimited objectives. The policy of the North was to restore the Union by force; the policy of the South was to establish its independence by force. Between these two purposes there could be no compromise, no halfway triumph for either side. One or the other had to achieve a complete and decisive victory.[1] Second, the Civil War

---

[1] The North's objectives could be obtained only by a total military victory. The South, on the other hand, could attain its objectives by preventing the North from winning such a victory. But the South's policy objectives were total; it could accept no result except independence.

was a war of matériel, bringing into full play for the first time the great transforming forces of the Industrial Revolution. Among the techniques and weapons employed—either used for the first time or given their first prominent use—were conscription and mass armies, mass production of weapons, railroads, armored ships, submarines, the telegraph, breech-loading and repeating rifles, various precursors of the machine gun, and an incipient air force in the form of signal balloons. Because of these distinguishing qualities the Civil War was, compared with earlier conflicts, a ruthless, lethal, no-holds-barred war. In the high command arrangements, especially in the North, it witnessed an unprecedented measure of civilian participation in strategic planning and of civilian direction of the war.

2

At the beginning of the war there were only two officers in the service who had ever commanded troops in numbers large enough to be called an army. One was Winfield Scott, who was seventy-five years of age, and the other was John E. Wool, who was two years older, and both of them had had their active experience in the Mexican War, when the largest field armies numbered about 14,000. Besides Scott and Wool, not an officer on either side had directed as large a unit as a brigade; only a few had commanded a regiment. The largest single army that the younger officers, the men who would become the generals of the war, had ever seen, except for the handful who had visited Europe, was Scott's or Taylor's force in the Mexican War. The 30,000 troops collected by the Federal government at Washington in the spring of 1861 were the largest single American army yet assembled. The photographs of Civil War generals tend to mislead us. We look at those fierce, bearded faces and think of the subjects as being old and hardened warriors. But despite the hirsute adornments, most of them were young men, and none of them, regardless of age, had ever handled troops in numbers before the war. This explains many of the mistakes made by both Northern and Southern generals in the early stages of the conflict. They were simply not prepared to direct the huge armies that were suddenly called into being and thrust upon them. The West Pointers, with the advantage of their technical training, were able to learn their jobs, but sometimes the educational process was painful—for them and their troops.

Both sides at first attempted to raise their armies by the traditional American method of calling for volunteers, and in the first year of the war, when both sections were moved by emotional outbursts of patriotism and optimistic estimates that the war would be of short duration, volunteering served to fill up the armies. But after the initial flush of enthusiasm had flickered out, enlistments dwindled away, and it became evident that the volunteer system would not supply enough men to constitute the huge armies the war was going to require. Both combatants had to

49

resort to conscription, the Confederate States in 1862 and the United States a year later—the first time in the American military experience that national conscription was employed. Because of faulty methods of keeping statistics the total number of men raised by either side can only be estimated. In the Confederacy 1,300,000 enlistments were counted, but this figure includes many short-term enlistments and duplicates. The same qualification must be made of the North's enlistment total of 2,900,000. The best estimates are that 1,500,000 men served in Federal armies for three years and 900,000 in Southern armies for the same period.

The field armies that appeared in the war dwarfed in size any force in previous American wars. Disregarding the many small army units that operated in various theaters, we will concern ourselves here with the maximum forces employed by North and South. In the Eastern theater the Federal Army of the Potomac varied from a minimum of 90,000 to a maximum of 130,000. The highest number attained by its opponent, the Army of Northern Virginia, was 85,000, but the average size of this force was smaller, ranging between 55,000 and 70,000. The largest Federal army in the West comprised 90,000 troops, while the biggest army which the Confederacy placed in the field in this theater numbered 70,000, a total far above the average, which ranged between 40,000 and 60,000.

The generals who commanded the large field armies were without exception professional soldiers, graduates of West Point. A large number of citizen soldiers in both armies proved themselves capable of directing divisions and corps, but the few amateurs who were given command of even small independent armies—as Benjamin F. Butler and N. P. Banks—were unequal to the task; N. B. Forrest on the Confederate side was a natural genius who probably could have led an army, but in actual experience he commanded only a cavalry force. It was the professionals, then, who in the area of battle operations fought the war and, for the North, won it. But it would be highly inaccurate to conclude from this that the trained experts demonstrated a consistent level of competence or manifested an immediate and perceptive awareness of the nature of modern war.

On the contrary, most of the Northern generals who came to prominence in the first half of the war were sorry field leaders—were, in fact, unfit for high level command. They exhibited a number of excellent qualities: they knew how—or, more accurately, they readily learned how—to prepare, train, and administer armies. There was only one quality that they lacked, but it was a fatal inadequacy: they did not want to fight their armies. In the first of the modern wars, in a war that both sides were playing for keeps, they were ruled by the military concepts of the eighteenth century. They thought of war as an exercise in bloodless strategy, as a series of maneuvers to checkmate an enemy on a gigantic chessboard. Above all—and here George B. McClellan is the supreme example of the type—they envisioned a leisurely, gentlemanly kind of war; in short, a war of limited objectives: if you don't accomplish your objective this time, all right, try it again later, next month, next year. McClellan always saw the war as a kind of game practiced by himself and other experts off in a private sphere of action that had no connection with the political community. If the public demanded action, if the government might fall because there was no action, such considerations impressed McClellan not at all. Ignorant politicians and other people should not be interfering with the specialists, who would move when the conditions of the game were exactly right and not one minute before.

Generals like McClellan were simply not competent to command in a conflict like the Civil War—a rough, mean war and one in which, whether the military liked it or not, civilians were going to have their say. Instead of recognizing the reality of civilian interference and accommodating himself to it, McClellan wasted his energies by wailing that it should not exist —the same kind of futile protest that his supporters have advanced ever since. Not until 1864 did the North succeed in bringing into the important command posts, in the persons of U. S. Grant, William T. Sherman, Philip H. Sheridan, and George H. Thomas, men who possessed the hard, driving qualities required in modern war and who understood the political nature of the war. Although the South owned its share of fumbling generals, it can be said of most Confederate commanders that, from the beginning, they were at least willing to fight their armies. Doubtless the inferior human and material resources of the South, which compelled her generals to act when they could with what they had, explains their greater aggressiveness.

3

At the outbreak of war neither side had ready at hand a plan of general strategy. The newly formed Confederate government could hardly have been expected to possess a previously devised design, but such a measure of preparation was well within the capacities of the Federal military organization. That no plan existed is, of course, not surprising. Nobody had thought, until the crisis suddenly broke, that the difficulties between the sections would come to war, and—here is the crux of the matter—nobody or any agency in the military system, neither Scott nor the General Staff, was charged with the function of studying strategy or of preparing plans for a possible war. The strategy of the war, then, had to be worked out as the conflict developed in the light of what the planners on each side could learn about the strategic situation. So far as prior preparations were concerned, neither government approached the standards of President Polk and his cabinet, who had outlined a general plan of operations a year before the war with Mexico started.[2]

[2] The several statements in these essays calling attention to the absence of plans at the beginning of wars are not to be taken as a belief in the necessity or feasibility of having a previously drawn up and detailed scheme of operations. Indeed, the possession of a rigid design may handicap a nation, as the experience of Germany with the Schlieffen plan attests. Especially today, when the nature of war is so fluid, it may be advantageous to be able to choose among a number of plans after war begins. What I am saying here is that in some of our wars *no thinking* about what might happen had been done before the advent of hostilities.

The policy of the North, or the United States, was to restore the Union by force; hence, Northern strategy had to be offensive. But the strategic objectives of the North were complicated by the fact that this was a civil instead of a foreign war. If it was to win, the North had to do more than occupy the enemy capital or defeat enemy armies. It had to do these things and, in addition, convince the Southern people that their cause was hopeless. In short, to conquer a peace the North had to subdue a population. Northern armies would have to invade the South, seize key points and areas, and occupy large regions of the enemy country —all of which would require a vast expenditure of human and military resources. Northern strategy, as it was finally formulated, set up three principal objectives to be attained: (1) in the Eastern theater to capture Richmond and defeat the defending Confederate army; (2) to seize the line of the Mississippi River, thereby splitting the Confederacy into two parts; and (3) after the second objective had been achieved, to occupy Chattanooga and the Tennessee River line, thereby gaining a base from which an offensive could be launched to divide the South, east of the Mississippi.

The policy of the Confederacy was to establish its independence by force, and to accomplish this purpose the government decided on a defensive strategy. In part, the South had no choice in the matter; its decision was a forced reaction to Northern strategy. But the adoption of a defensive strategy was also in part a deliberate determination by its leaders, particularly by President Davis. For a power that wanted only to be let alone and that harbored no aggressive designs against anybody, a strategy of defense seemed so beautifully logical—and Confederates were always beguiled by logic. But because the South's only purpose was to resist conquest was not sufficient reason to rely on such an inert strategy. With equal logic, and probably with more effect, the South might have achieved its policy of independence by taking the offensive early in the war when its resources were greatest, by demonstrating that it was too strong to be conquered through victories on Northern soil.

Confederate strategy was pervasively and, in a sense, passively defensive. The high command decided to defend every part of the Confederacy, to meet every threatened attack, to hold every threatened point— a policy which dispersed its resources, inferior to those of the North, over a wide strategic circumference and yielded the strategic initiative to the enemy.[3] If the South chose to await attack, it might have adopted an alternative defensive strategy; it could have shortened its lines to inclose the most defensible areas or those containing important resources or possessing a symbolic value. It did not do this, partly for valid reasons. For the new Southern government to abandon any of its territory would have seemed an admission of weakness and would certainly have lost it a measure of popular support. But even without these practical

[3] It is recognized, of course, that on occasion the Confederacy did go over to the offensive, as in Bragg's invasion of Kentucky in 1862 and, most notably, in Lee's thrusts into the North in 1862 and 1863. But these operations were exceptions to the rule. Also, in every case where an offensive was attempted, the size of the Confederate army could have been significantly augmented by adding to it forces that were guarding places at home.

political considerations, President Davis and other civil leaders seemed to think almost instinctively in terms of defending places for their own sake, of holding territory simply because it was their territory.

In general, at the highest command levels the North displayed a greater degree of efficiency and originality than did the South. The Confederates, so brilliant in tactical maneuvers and in battlefield strategy, never succeeded in creating a competent command system or in setting up a unified plan of strategy. The Northern strategy of offense was basically sound; the Southern strategy of defense was fundamentally defective. But it would be inaccurate and unfair to ascribe the differences between the strategic systems to the human beings who operated them, to say that one side had wise leaders and the other had not, to dismiss Davis and his advisers as inept and unintelligent men (as a matter of fact, they were very intelligent) who did not rise to their opportunities. Warfare should always be considered a social institution. As Clausewitz said, a nation's social system or culture will determine the kind of war it will fight. Davis and Lee and other Confederates were the products of their culture, and their culture decided and limited their military thinking. Whereas, the North was a nation of the nineteenth century and looked to the future, the South was a confederation of sovereignties that refused to accept the nineteenth century and looked to the past. The Confederacy was founded on state rights—localism was imbedded in every segment of its system—and it fought a state-rights war and, on the strategic level, a traditional, eighteenth-century type of war. Just as it was difficult for Southern political leaders to envision centralism in government, so it was hard for Confederate military directors to see the war as a whole or to install centralism in its direction.

4

At the head of the military systems of both countries and of their command organizations were the two presidents, Abraham Lincoln and Jefferson Davis. They form an interesting contrast and offer the materials for an instructive and fascinating study in civil-military relationships and in the higher direction of war. Judging them solely by their backgrounds, one would expect that the Confederate President would be a great war leader, that he would far eclipse his rival. Few civilian war directors have come to their office with Davis' technical advantages. He was a graduate of West Point, he had served in the regular army, he had had battle experience in the Mexican War, and he had been Secretary of War. Lincoln had been a civilian all his life, he had received no military education, and he had had no military experience except briefly as a militia soldier in the Black Hawk War, when, as he liked to recall, he had made some ferocious charges on the wild onions and engaged in bloody struggles with the mosquitoes. And yet the truth is that Lincoln was a great war president and Davis was a mediocre one. The command careers of the two men illustrate perfectly the truth of Clause-witz' dictum that an acquaintance with military affairs is not the principal qualification for a direc-tor of war but that "a remarkable, superior mind and strength of character" are more important.

We cannot pause here to measure Davis' defects as a political leader of his people, intriguing though such an analysis of this sincere and tormented man would be. But certainly the weaknesses that he dis-played—his excessive pride, his sensitivity to criticism, his impatience of contradiction, his lack of passion for anything, even for the South—detracted from his effectiveness as President and contributed to the final defeat of the Southern cause. We are concerned with his qualities as a war director, and we are ob-liged to note that in this area he failed as surely as he did in the political sphere.

He failed because he did not seem to realize what his task was or what his proper functions were. He could not grasp the vital fact that the Confederacy was not a going, recognized government but a revolu-tion and that, in order to win, it would have to act with remorseless revolutionary vigor. Always he pro-ceeded on the theory that the Confederacy was a permanent government and could act like older estab-lished governments, and always he observed every nicety of legal punctilio and tied himself up in every possible piece of red tape. Because of his military back-ground, he fancied himself a military expert; he would rather have been a general than the head of state. Somebody in our own times has quipped that Davis learned enough about war in a few minutes at Buena Vista in the Mexican War to defeat the South; and during the war Richmond wags, referring to Davis' boasting about a formation he had led at Buena Vista, said that the Confederacy was dying of an inverted V. His image of himself being what it was, he concerned himself overly much with military affairs. The criticism here is not that he interfered with his generals—this point will be discussed later—but that he spent too much time on unimportant routine items, on matters that he should have left to subordinates. Once he even proposed to go through 1,500 documents bearing on promotions high and low. He could not delegate authority to people he knew were not as competent as he. Because he was a capable administrator, he loved to do the administrating himself. He had been an outstanding Secretary of War, but as President he rarely rose above the secretarial level.

Nor can we take time to analyze the qualities that made Lincoln a great war President. They are so well known, perhaps, that they do not need repetition. We may note two factors, however, that reveal something of his concept of the role of commander-in-chief and that help to explain his success as a war director. First, Lincoln was, in a technical sense, a poor administrator. Unlike Davis, who spent much time in his office, Lincoln was rarely in his office. He was often to be found in the offices of other people, generals and secretaries, ostensibly visiting around and telling stories, but really sizing up subordinates and deciding whether he could delegate authority to them. When he found a man whom he could trust to do a job, Lincoln was quite willing to let him handle the details of his office. In short, he was interested in the big administrative picture, and he did not, if he could avoid it, burden himself with petty routine—all of which means that he understood perfectly his function and the proper function of administration (or if he did not understand good administration, he intuitively practiced it). Second, Lincoln realized immediately that the war was a revolution, and he dealt with it on that basis. Whenever he felt that revolutionary methods were necessary to attain the objectives of Union policy, he used them, even to the length of violating law or the Constitution. He was not, he explained, going to see the government and the nation go to smash because of a squeamish regard for legal niceties. It is a curious fact that Lincoln, who headed an established government, acted with more revolutionary zeal than Davis, who led an experimental government.

As a director of war Lincoln displayed, almost from the beginning, a fine strategic sense. He was a better natural strategist than were most of his generals who were trained soldiers. Grasping the importance of economic warfare, he proclaimed a naval blockade of the South. Realizing that numbers were on his side, he called for 400,000 volunteers in 1861. Almost immediately he understood one of the great all-time strategic maxims, which his first generals seem never to have heard of, and applied it to his war: the proper objective of Union armies, he insisted, was the destruction of Confederate armies and not the occupation of Southern territory. Knowing the advantage that superior forces gave the North, he disregarded the traditional Jomini doctrine of concentrating at one point, and showing a startling originality in his strategic thinking, he urged his commanders to keep up a constant pressure on the whole strategic line of the Confederacy until a weak spot was found and a break-through could be made. Always, always, he prodded the generals to move, to execute an offensive strategy.

Both Lincoln and Davis have been criticized by historians and military writers for "interfering" with generals and military affairs. Most of these strictures seem misinformed. Judged by modern standards both presidents did some things that a civil director of war should not do. But it must be emphasized that they were operating without benefit of a formal command system, that they executed functions which, in the organization then existing, could have been performed by no other agency. Moreover, if the caliber of many of the generals, the so-called trained experts, is carefully measured, it is evident that the presidents were often justified in the supervision they exerted. Particularly for the Union cause, as will be demonstrated later, it was fortunate that Lincoln called his generals to account. But the vital point about such "interfering" is the purpose for which the war director intervenes—the strategic objective he is trying to accomplish. If the strategy is sound and if the director of war is a man of "a remarkable, su-perior mind," the results of his intervention will be generally good. Lincoln interfered to make a sound offensive strategy stronger, and Davis interfered to make a defective defensive strategy more defensive. One acted from a valid theory and the other from a faulty one.

5

In describing the machinery of the command arrangements of both sides, we will consider first the organization of the Confederate system, giving it relatively brief attention, not because in the history of the war it was less important than its Northern counterpart but because, unlike the latter, it contributed little to the development of modern concepts of command.

The formal organization of the Confederate military system was practically identical with that of the United States. The President acted as commander-in-chief of the armed forces, assisted by two civilian deputies, the secretaries of War and the Navy. Davis permitted his naval secretary a relatively free hand, but he supervised the War office with minute care. Something of his interest in this department is revealed by the number of men, five, who passed through its organization as Secretary; Davis was, in reality, his own Secretary of War. To assist the President and Secretary in administering the housekeeping branches of the army, the Confederate Congress authorized the establishment of a number of staff or bureau agencies—quartermaster general, adjutant general, and others—similar to the organs in the Northern General Staff.

Without being too inaccurate, one could summarize Confederate command arrangements by saying that they consisted mainly of President Davis. He was general-in-chief as well as commander-in-chief, and he attempted to exercise both functions to the fullest.

The most that he would permit his civil or military assistants to offer was advice—which, if they were smart, they offered only when asked. Early in 1862 Davis assigned R. E. Lee to Richmond to act "under the direction of the President" as commanding general of all Confederate forces. The phrases in the directive were impressive, but in practice Lee became a mere adviser who furnished his superior, when requested, with technical counsel. In the summer of 1862 Lee left the office to become field commander of the Army of Northern Virginia, and Davis did not name a successor until February, 1864. In the long interim Davis, acting without professional advice except that which he might choose to obtain from field commanders, formulated the basic strategy of the Confederacy. To the President's credit it should be noted that on at least one occasion he tried to delegate authority to a departmental commander. His plan, which was an interesting attempt to tighten up command arrangements, called for placing all armies in the Western theater under one general, Joseph E. Johnston, who, in modern parlance, would function as an army group commander. The experiment failed because Johnston refused to accept the responsibilities of his position.

In 1864, at a time when the government was under criticism after a series of disasters, Davis resurrected the office of General-in-Chief, naming to fill it Braxton Bragg, who as a field commander in the West had been responsible for many of the disasters. Public and political pressures had forced Davis to remove Bragg from field command, and his assignment of the general to service in Richmond may have been only a gesture of defiance to his critics and an affirmation of his confidence in Bragg. At any rate, Bragg, who possessed real ability in strategic planning, understood his position and his superior perfectly. He restricted his functions to providing requested advice and praising Davis' military wisdom. In February, 1865, the Confederate Congress, in a move designed to clip Davis' powers, formally created the office of General-in-Chief, and the sponsors of the measure made it plain that the post was intended for Lee and that Lee would be expected to direct the Confederacy's strategy and operations. Davis, having no choice, appointed Lee, but he announced that he was still the commander-in-chief and intended to continue. Lee, who had great respect for civil authority, accepted the commission on the basis offered by the President. The war ended before the new command experiment could be tested. It is doubtful whether Lee could have performed the dual functions of army commander and general-in-chief. Nor is it certain that Lee, who was a product of his culture and obsessed with the war in his native Virginia, could have adjusted his strategic thinking to the problems of national strategy on many fronts. The South did not achieve, and probably could not have achieved, a modern command system.[4]

---

[4] The best treatment of Confederate command arrangements is Frank E. Vandiver, *Rebel Brass: The Confederate Command System* (Baton Rouge, 1956).

6

Northern command arrangements at the highest level consisted in 1861 of General Scott, who was general-in-chief, and the General Staff, comprising the bureau heads in the War Department. The General Staff, we must emphasize again, was not a collective agency, was not concerned with strategy, and according to modern military usage was a misnamed body. In the first months of the war Lincoln turned to General Scott and other officers for advice on strategic questions. At this stage he was perhaps too much inclined to defer to the professionals and tended to exaggerate the potential of the military mind.

His first shock of disillusionment came when he asked Scott to present a plan of general strategy. The old general, who had done no previous thinking about strategy for the war, responded with a scheme that demonstrated he was unable to envision the requirements of modern mass war and was not the man to direct general operations. His so-called Anaconda Plan proposed a naval blockade of the Southern coastline and the occupation of the Mississippi River line by a combined land and naval force. These objectives secured and the South inclosed in an iron circle, Scott would stop and do nothing more, waiting for the squeeze of the blockade to bring an alleged Union sentiment in the besieged section to the surface, after which the South would voluntarily seek peace. Although the plan had obvious merits—the blockade and the occupation of the Mississippi became major items in Northern strategy—Lincoln rightly rejected it, partly because it would take too long to accomplish its by-no-means-certain results. But, more important, Lincoln the civilian recognized the fundamental defect in Scott's thinking. The soldier was advocating the one-idea type of strategy: one kind of operation, one weapon, one branch of the service will win the war.[5]

Partly at his own request, partly because of pressure from above, Scott retired from service on November 1, 1861, and to the post of General-in-Chief Lincoln named George B. McClellan, who was also the field commander of the Army of the Potomac. This is not the place to discuss McClellan's shortcomings as a battle captain, which were many and fatal, except as his qualities as a field general seem to be related to his course as general-in-chief. The one great defect that he displayed in both areas was an inability to see things as they were, to distinguish the actual factors in a situation from imagined ones. He lived much of the time in a world of fantasy of his own making. His incapacity to adjust his thinking to the realities was fully apparent in the one plan of general strategy he submitted to Lincoln. He proposed that an army of 273,000 (why he hit upon this rather odd number he did not explain) be assembled

[5] It may be said that this criticism of Scott, especially in view of his age and former services, is too harsh. In defense of Scott one may argue that such a move as he proposed, and particularly the blockade, was the only operation immediately feasible for the North and that few people in 1861 foresaw the frightful length and extent to which the war would go. On the other hand Scott, before the shooting started, had busied himself devising political plans to avert war, and it is evident that his mind was working in the direction of diplomatic or economic action instead of war.

in the Eastern theater to operate under his command. With the support of the navy he would land this force on the Virginia Coast, march inland, and capture Richmond. Then he would sail down the coast and repeat the process with other important Southern cities, finally ending up at New Orleans. It was about as fantastic a proposal as Lincoln received from a military man, and he was to be the recipient of many.

On many counts the plan was defective. It concentrated operations in one theater to the neglect of others and it made places instead of armies the objectives. Worst of all, it was too grandiose to be supported by existing resources. At that time the government could not have collected so many troops in one theater and housed and fed them, nor did it have sufficient sea transport to carry them to McClellan's points of attack. And even if all these conditions could have been met, McClellan did not possess the staff organization to administer such a host. This incredible design, which must have astounded Lincoln and which he filed without comment, confirmed his developing doubts of the capacities of military men.

With the exception of this proposal McClellan offered no strategic suggestions worthy of Lincoln's consideration or our attention. During the winter of 1861–62 he was busy preparing his field army for operations in the spring. Whatever plans of strategy were advanced came from the President, who vainly urged McClellan and other field commanders to deliver simultaneous attacks along the entire strategic line of the Confederacy. This idea, which was eminently sound and which was the strategy eventually adopted by the North, was received

67

with scorn by the generals, partly because it was the proposal of a civilian and partly because it violated the traditional Jomini concept of concentration at one point. On several occasions during the winter Lincoln prodded McClellan to undertake even a minor or diversionary movement to sustain popular morale, to demonstrate to the public that the armies meant business. That he refused was characteristic of McClellan and of the military tradition he represented. War was a game played by professionals and had no relation to political requirements; he would move when the game was right. It was also characteristic of McClellan that, when he did decide on a spring movement for his own army, he did not, for months, inform Lincoln of his plan. He did not seem to know how to form such a relationship with his civilian superior that he could counsel with him on strategy; in fact, he did not seem to realize that he ought to offer any guidance to his superior.

When McClellan took the field in March, 1862, Lincoln removed him as general-in-chief, presumably on the grounds that one man could not direct a field army and at the same time plan movements for other armies. The President did not immediately name a successor to McClellan. For approximately five months he left the position vacant, during which time he acted as his own general-in-chief. It may be surmised that Lincoln either had decided he could perform the function of directing strategy himself or that he was looking around for a suitable officer for the place. During this period he detached McDowell's corps from McClellan's army to insure the safety of Washington, planned the offensive movement in the Shen-

GENERAL GEORGE WASHINGTON

Washington was selected to command the American forces in the Revolution for a combination of reasons. He had had extensive military experience in the Virginia militia; he was a wealthy man and would add a tone of conservatism to the patriotic cause, and he was a Southerner whose appointment would militate against the feeling that the war was a New England affair. Lacking a formal military education, Washington had many things to learn about war. But he had the capacity to learn and developed into an extremely competent general. Undoubtedly he was the best man that could have been picked for the supreme command.

JAMES MADISON

Chief Executive during the War of 1812, Madison was the first war-time President. Learned, humane, amiable, he occupies an honored place in our history. But he was not an effective director of war. Although he bustled around frequently to the War and Naval departments, he did not really act as commander-in-chief. His talents were not fitted for war, and he was unable to run the military machine.

JOHN ARMSTRONG

Armstrong saw service as an officer in the Revolution. A Republican politician from New York, he was named Secretary of War in 1813 partly to give a non-Virginia flavor to the Madison administration. Pugnacious by nature, he added to his troubles as a member of the administration by openly professing contempt for Virginians. The first wartime Secretary, he brought a much-needed energy into the direction of the War Department. But he displayed a faulty sense of administration by trying to exercise functions foreign to his office.

GENERAL WINFIELD SCOTT

Joining the army as a young man right before the War of 1812, Scott remained in the service until he retired as an old man in 1861. For twenty years he was commanding general. Few men have left a deeper or more enduring impress on the army. His Mexican War campaign entitles him to be ranked just outside the select group of great American soldiers. But because of his age and because his experience had been with small armies, he probably could not have adjusted himself to the new kind of war beginning in 1861.

JAMES K. POLK

Polk was the first President to function actively as commander-in-chief. He supervised minutely every phase of the war with Mexico, sometimes carrying his control to extreme lengths. But whatever mistakes he committed—and his judgment of men and measures was not always of the best—he demonstrated that a President could act as commander-in-chief. Driving himself relentlessly while in office, he died soon after returning to his Tennessee home.

LINCOLN AND McCLELLAN

The two principal command figures of the first phase of the Civil War confront each other in McClellan's headquarters tent after the battle of Antietam. Lincoln often visited generals in the field to get a firsthand impression. It may have been after this trip that Lincoln uttered his classic summary of McClellan. Somebody had said the general was a fine military engineer. This was true, Lincoln agreed, but he seemed to have a special talent for a stationary engine.

General Ulysses S. Grant

One observer has said that Grant looked as though he could butt his head through a brick wall and was about to do so. Long underrated by military students, he is just now beginning to receive recognition as a great general. As general-in-chief in 1864, he demonstrated that he could take an over-all view of strategy. Unlike McClellan and many other generals on both sides, he was a modern soldier.

General Emory Upton

Even when he was a cadet at West Point, Upton was known as a scholar and a person with strong opinions. He never changed his character nor his interests. Graduating in 1861, he was immediately caught up in the Civil War. His war career was varied and distinguished. He saw service in the artillery, infantry, and cavalry, and rose to divisional command. Although a meticulous soldier, Upton did not hesitate to criticize his superiors when he thought the occasion warranted. After the war his scholarly qualities were recognized by the army. Assigned to study foreign armies and encouraged to write, he produced several books. His *The Military Policy of the United States* is probably the most influential book ever written by an American soldier. Packed with facts, its value as a historical document is, however, questionable because of its dubious thesis.

RUSSELL A. ALGER

Alger was a Michigan businessman and politician. He had been a volunteer officer in the Civil War, eventually commanding a regiment. But his appointment as Secretary of War in 1897 was a political reward, not a recognition of his fitness for the post. He was a kindly man, but he had no great strength of character and no particular ability for administration. Much of what happened in his department during the War with Spain would have occurred no matter who had been Secretary, but he did little to control events. He resigned in 1899 at President McKinley's request.

WILLIAM McKINLEY

McKinley may be characterized as the politicians' politician—a near perfect example of the species. Warm, friendly, lovable, he excelled in the individual conference and in the art of adjustment. As President he restored to the office some of the prestige it had lost since the Civil War. He did this not by defying Congress but by manipulating it. He was a manager rather than a leader of men. His talents did not equip him to be a great war President; he tended to avoid the big decision that only he could make.

ELIHU ROOT

In any listing of the great Secretaries of War, Root would hold a high place. Coming into office at a critical moment in the army's history, he pushed through a series of measures that revitalized the land forces. Undoubtedly Root was too much inclined to minimize the American military experience and to scorn the American talent for improvisation. But while the value of the Root reforms has been exaggerated by many commentators, the net effect of the Secretary's work was to give the nation a more effective military system.

GENERAL JOHN J. PERSHING

In World War I Pershing had the experience of serving as commander of the American army before the relationship between the ranking field general and the Chief of Staff had been clarified. In Pershing's view the function of the latter officer, Peyton March, was to minister to the needs of the army in France. In March's view, Pershing was a subordinate to be directed from Washington. The result of their different interpretations was almost constant controversy. Not until the eve of World War II was the command status of the Chief of Staff made clear and specific.

NEWTON D. BAKER

Among the martial figures of World War I Baker seemed strangely out of place. He was prim in appearance and had been known as a pacifist. A lawyer and a politician, he had had little administrative experience before becoming Secretary of War. Highly intelligent, he caught on readily to the routine of his job and performed competently. Perhaps his most difficult function was mediating the command controversy between Generals Pershing and March.

GENERAL PEYTON C. MARCH

The Chief of Staff in World War I, March was a dedicated soldier. His concept of his command position embroiled him in almost constant bickering with Pershing. In the Pershing circle it was fashionable to compare him with Halleck in the Civil War. The analogy was false and illustrates the faulty knowledge of American military history held by most soldiers of the war, including March, and by many of their civilian colleagues as well.

GENERAL GEORGE C. MARSHALL   *Courtesy of the National Archives*

MILITARY LEADERS OF WORLD WAR II

Two key figures in American command arrangements in World War II were President Franklin D. Roosevelt and General George C. Marshall, Chief of Staff of the army, who enjoyed Roosevelt's almost complete confidence. Even yet historians are not agreed on the extent of Roosevelt's role as commander-in-chief nor on the nature of his relations with Marshall and the other staff heads comprising the Joint Chiefs of Staff. According to one view, Roosevelt was a somewhat passive war director, concerned only with winning the war quickly and largely reliant on the advice of his top military assistants.

Professor Samuel P. Huntington, in *The Soldier and the State* (Cambridge, 1957), states flatly that "the military ran the war." Some critics of this school contend that the military men had no concept of war as an instrument of policy, pointing as proof to Marshall's statement: "I would be loath to hazard American lives for purely political purposes." But Professor Huntington thinks that the Joint Chiefs, in pursuing the objective of a purely military triumph, were but reflecting the goal of the policy or civilian agency. That is, they conformed to the common American idea of war—the object of war is total victory, not postwar security.

FRANKLIN D. ROOSEVELT   *Courtesy of the National Archives*

MILITARY LEADERS OF WORLD WAR II

Another view comes from Professor William Emerson in an article, "Franklin Roosevelt as Commander-in-Chief in World War II," in *Military Affairs* (Winter, 1958–1959). Emerson concedes that Roosevelt did not exercise such a control over the war machine as Winston Churchill did in Great Britain and that the American Joint Chiefs enjoyed more autonomy than did their British counterparts. Nevertheless, says Emerson, the picture of the passive Roosevelt is deceiving. When the President wanted to, he could intervene in military affairs powerfully and decisively. The apparent harmony between Roosevelt and his chiefs did not mean that the latter were running the show. Rather, the chiefs often knew in advance what Roosevelt's views were and adapted to them. Nor, according to Emerson, was Roosevelt insensitive to the political ends of war. He wanted to win the war in such a way as not to commit the United States to postwar burdens in Europe.

Whatever the merits of the case, it would seem that Roosevelt proceeded in a manner typically American. His war arrangements were like everything he did. Secretary Stimson said that as an administrator Roosevelt was "inherently disorderly." This is another way of saying that he possessed the national talent for improvisation.

andoah Valley to trap Stonewall Jackson, and combined the separate armies in northern Virginia under the single command of John Pope. He not only framed strategy but on several occasions, as when he instructed one general on the proper use of signal fires, he got down to the tactical level. Some of his decisions were wise, others were open to criticism. Generally, his basic concepts were sound. When he erred, it was because he sometimes found difficulty in expressing his strategic notions in terms that the military mind could understand or because, as in the Valley campaign, he minimized logistical factors and exaggerated the strategic possibilities of a situation. And, it should be added, he asked too much of some very dull generals.

It must not be supposed, however, that Lincoln was running a one-man show, making decisions right and left without consultation. He conferred regularly with his executive deputy, Secretary of War Edwin M. Stanton, and other War Department officials. In the Civil War, for the first time, the civilian division of the department was placed on an adequate administrative basis. With three assistant secretaries authorized by Congress, the department was no longer an assemblage of clerks but a professional agency. Moreover, Secretary Stanton infused new importance into the bureau system. He set up an organ known as the Army Board, which consisted of the various bureau heads and was presided over by General E. A. Hitchcock. Although this was only the General Staff under another name, a forward step had been taken. The staff now had a chairman and could act as a collective body. Its members were not qualified to rule on matters of general strategy, but they were

69

competent to advise on lesser strategic issues and to offer technical information. Lincoln frequently went to the War Department to talk with the Army Board before coming to a decision.

Whatever doubts Lincoln had come to have about professional soldiers, whatever convictions of growing strategic powers were stirring in his mind, he resolved to have one more try at intrusting the direction of strategic operations to a general. Perhaps he sensed that he, a civilian, was exercising too much control over the conduct of the war. In July, 1862, he called General Henry W. Halleck to Washington from the West and appointed him general-in-chief. Halleck seemed to be an ideal choice for the position. A graduate of West Point with long years of service in the regular army, he was known before the war as one of the few and one of the foremost American students of the higher art of war—of strategy and military history. Most of the great books on war had been written in French by such masters as Napoleon and Jomini, and only a handful of American officers had enough facility with the French language to read them. Halleck, a linguistic scholar, had translated several of these works and had written a book of his own on war, *Elements of Military Art and Science,* which followed Jomini closely. Even after he became general-in-chief, Halleck continued to interpret Jomini's writings, causing one of his critics to jibe that "General Halleck is translating French books at nine cents a page; and sir, if you should put those nine cents in a box and shake them up, you would form a clear idea of General Halleck's soul." (Jomini, with his doctrine of concentration at one point, had an enormous influence on Civil War strategists; Mc-Clellan's proposal to mass 273,000 men in one theater was a Jomini concept.[6]) In addition to theoretical knowledge, Halleck had another apparent qualification for supreme command: he seemed to be a successful general. Under his command in the Western department a number of victories, the first Union successes of the war, had been won. They had been won by other generals, notably by U. S. Grant, without Halleck having had much to do with them, but the departmental commander received the credit.

Lincoln installed Halleck in the office with the full intention that the general should function as actual general-in-chief, that is, with the President's approval,

[6] Because of the several critical references to Jomini in this essay, it is necessary, to avoid being unfair to him, to qualify some of my statements. At no point have I meant to imply that there is any contradiction between Jomini's concept of concentration and offensive action. He realized fully the advantage of the offensive. Although at times he advocated the destruction of enemy armies, at others he recommended the occupation of places, and it was the latter objective which his American admirers adopted. Nor have I meant to argue that there may not be times in war when massive concentration at one point may not be decisive. It may be, especially in relatively small countries like those in Europe to which Jomini applied his doctrines. It may be doubted, however, that one big breakthrough by the North would have collapsed the South. The point made here is that several simultaneous attacks, which the North was well able to mount, constituted the best strategy for the side with the superior resources. But the Northern generals tended to insist, using Jomini's principle of concentration, that only one big effort should be made at a time, meaning, of course, by one army—their particular army. It can be argued that Jomini's concepts were not intrinsically faulty but that his American followers were misinterpreting them.

71

should plan and direct over-all strategy. Lincoln meant to keep his own hands off the details of military administration. When commanders in various departments wrote Lincoln asking for instructions, he referred them to Halleck who, he said, now had charge of the entire field. At first Halleck carried out the responsibilities of his job, but within less than two months he experienced a mental and military breakdown and refused to exercise his functions. Fundamentally Halleck was unfit for the post of General-in-Chief because he disliked to assume responsibility. He loved to offer advice and technical criticism to the President or to field generals, but he flinched from making flat decisions or issuing definite instructions. In August after the Union defeat in the battle of Second Manassas, he almost collapsed. His was an impossible position he felt; to the field general went the credit for a victory, but upon the general-in-chief fell the blame for all failures. Therefore, he abnegated the duties of his office and deliberately assumed the role of a mere adviser. When Lincoln asked him for counsel, he furnished it, but he would do nothing more. When the President asked him to go to the Army of the Potomac, survey the situation, and order what should be done, Halleck replied that if he had to shoulder such a responsibility he would resign.

Halleck's refusal to execute the duties of his position forced Lincoln to resume the functions of general-in-chief, which he would perform until the early months of 1864. Although the President was disappointed in Halleck, he continued to keep him in the post of commanding general. He retained

Halleck because he needed somebody near him who could provide technical military information and advice. In addition, he discovered that Halleck was extremely valuable as a medium of communication with the military. Often Lincoln and his generals failed to understand each other because, almost literally, they did not speak the same language. Lincoln, speaking the terminology of the lawyer and the politician, could not always frame his strategic concepts, particularly in writing, in words that the soldiers could grasp. The generals, using the jargon peculiar to their profession, could not always describe their plans in terms the President could understand. Halleck had associated so much with civilians and soldiers that he could speak the language of both and was able to explain Lincoln's ideas to the generals and translate the generals' notions to Lincoln. As Halleck became increasingly adept at formulating Lincoln's thoughts, the President intrusted to him more and more the framing of military directives. Lincoln did not, however, often turn to the general-in-chief for strategic counsel. In the planning of several important movements Halleck does not seem to have been consulted; apparently he first learned of General Joseph Hooker's crossing of the Rappahannock in the opening campaign of 1863 from a chance encounter with an officer on the streets in Washington.

In late 1862 and during 1863, when Lincoln was acting as his own general-in-chief, he had undoubtedly come to have something of a scorn for professional soldiers. Whereas in the first days of the war he had been too much inclined to defer to their opinions, he had passed to the opposite extreme of being too ready to impose his opinions on them. He had seen too many of his generals plead excuse after excuse for not fighting: they needed more men and then more supplies and then more transportation—and then they would start the whole cycle over again. He had urged too many of his generals to seek the final decision of battle, to make enemy armies instead of places their objective, only to see them shrink from the decision, to see them place the occupation of territory above the destruction of the enemy's forces. Always growing in stature as a strategist, Lincoln loomed high in ability above most of the generals whom he was forced to use. We may now examine some of his "interferences" with commanders and note what the effects on the Union cause would have been if he had not intervened when he did.

In the summer of 1863 General Lee started his Confederate army west from Fredericksburg to the Shenandoah Valley and then headed north toward the Potomac. This was the beginning of the offensive that would culminate in the battle of Gettysburg. North of the Rappahannock Federal General Hooker studied the movements of the man who had defeated him at Chancellorsville, and he soon divined that Lee was aiming an invasion at Maryland or Pennsylvania. The reactions of the trained soldier were almost incredible. First he proposed to Lincoln that he cross the river and attack Lee's rear area forces at Fredericksburg. When the President vetoed this scheme, Hooker came up with an even wilder one. Contending that the government should be able to collect a sufficient force of reserves to halt Lee, he asked for permission to take his army south to attack Richmond. In rejecting this plan, Lincoln pointed out the obvious. Hooker would shatter his strength against the Richmond defenses while Lee ranged through Pennsylvania without opposition. And even if Hooker captured the Southern capital, its possession would not compensate for the prestige the Confederacy would gain, especially in Europe, by a successful offensive into the North. Hooker's proper move, Lincoln instructed, was to move his army to a position where it could fight Lee, which was what Hooker, at the President's direction, finally did.

At the battle of Gettysburg, General George G. Meade, who succeeded Hooker as commander of the Army of the Potomac, threw back Lee's attacks and hurt the Confederate army badly. Meade had fought a skillful defensive battle, but he was satisfied with his victory as it was. He was content to see Lee leave his front, and his principal concern was to "herd" Lee back over the Potomac. Like other Federal generals, he lacked the killer instinct, which all the great battle captains have had, to finish off the enemy. After the engagement he issued a congratulatory order to his troops in which he praised them for having driven the enemy from "our soil." After all, this was a civil war! When Lincoln read the order, he exclaimed in anguish, "My God! Is that all?" The President saw more clearly than his commander the results of Gettysburg: the Confederate army had been dealt a murderous blow and a decisive attack on it north of the Potomac might complete its destruction. He also sensed that Meade shrank from delivering such an attack, and through Halleck he urged Meade to pursue Lee and finish him off. But Meade merely followed his retreating foe and, even though Lee was held up by high water at the Potomac, permitted him to escape. Weeks later the general came to Washington for conferences, and during a conversation Lincoln said to him suddenly, "Do you know, general, what your attitude towards Lee for a week after the battle reminded me of?" "No, Mr. President, what is it?" asked Meade. "I'll be hanged if I could think of anything else," said Lincoln, "than an old woman trying to shoo her geese across a creek." As an analysis of Meade's psychology, this was perfect.

During the siege of Vicksburg Lincoln was beset by fears that the Confederates might detach troops from their army in eastern Tennessee to reinforce the Southern field army in Mississippi for an attack on Grant's rear. To protect Grant and to prevent the siege of the vital river fortress from being lifted, Lincoln asked General W. S. Rosecrans, the Federal commander in Tennessee, to mount an offensive to contain the Confederate army in Tennessee. Rosecrans replied with the kind of analysis of the situation that Lincoln often received from his generals and that made him think soldiers were maybe, as he put it, "a little crazy." The general said that it would be unwise for him to undertake a forward movement, because if he moved he would only push the Confederates closer to Mississippi. His proper course, he explained, was to sit where he was, do nothing, and occupy the enemy's attention. In all of Rosecrans' correspondence with the President there was one possibility that he never discussed, that he did not even seem to consider. Like so many of Lincoln's generals in a crisis, it did not occur to him that he might advance and win a victory. Ultimately he did move, but, like Hooker, because the President made him.

7

Although Lincoln wielded his great powers as war director with a certainty that came from ever growing confidence, he was willing, as he had always indicated, to yield those powers to a general who was competent and willing to exercise them. By 1864 he had found his man—and Congress and the nation ratified the choice—in U. S. Grant, who in the West had emerged as the greatest Union general of the war. In February Congress created the rank of lieutenant general, expressing a wish that Grant would receive the grade and the position of General-in-Chief, and Lincoln unhesitatingly named Grant to both. At last the United States was about to get a modern command system.

In the system arrived at in 1864, which was the joint product of Lincoln, Grant, and maybe of Halleck, Grant as general-in-chief was charged with the functions of framing over-all Union strategy and directing the movements of all Federal armies. As commanding general, Grant might have been expected to establish his command post in Washington, where he would be near the President and in quick contact with Federal field generals all over the country. But Grant disliked the political atmosphere of the capital, and he set up his headquarters with the Army of the Potomac in the field. He was always close to Washington, which he could reach in a short train trip, and he was in almost instant telegraphic communication with the President. Technically, Grant did not become commander of the Eastern field army—Meade continued to hold that position—but since he traveled with that army, it was subject to his close supervision.

Under the new arrangement Halleck received a new command office, the Chief of Staff. Again, as when we dealt with the nature of the General Staff, we must avoid confusion between nineteenth-century and contemporary usages of the same term. Halleck was not a chief of staff in the modern sense. In the present command system his position would correspond perhaps to the Secretary of the General Staff. Primarily he was a channel of communication between Lincoln and Grant and between Grant and the seventeen departmental commanders under the general-in-chief. Grant sent most of his dispatches for the President to Halleck, who, when necessary, briefed or explained them for Lincoln. Similarly, Halleck transmitted to Grant many of Lincoln's directives or inquiries concerning strategic matters. Because of Halleck's facility in the languages of both soldier and civilian, Lincoln and Grant never misunderstood each other, as Lincoln and McClellan so often had.

Halleck also served as a liaison between Grant and the department and field commanders. If Grant had had to read all the reports from these officers and frame detailed instructions for them, he would not have had much time for strategic planning. At Grant's direction, the subordinate commanders sent their dispatches for Grant to Halleck, who either transmitted them to the general-in-chief or summarized their contents for him. Grant sent most of his orders to subordinates through Halleck. Often he would tell the chief of staff in general terms what he wanted done and ask him to put the objective in a written directive, or he would delegate authority to Halleck to handle a particular situation. Although Halleck professed to think that his role in the command system was insignificant, it was really vitally important. Without such a coordinator of information the system would not have worked as brilliantly as it did.

But the key military man in the system was Grant. As general-in-chief, he proved to be the general for whom Lincoln had been searching. And because the President came to realize Grant's capacities, he gave him more latitude in determining strategy than he had permitted McClellan or Halleck. To a man who asked whether Grant did not have too much freedom of decision, Lincoln said, "Do you hire a man to do your work and then do it yourself?" Grant possessed the rare ability to see the war as a total picture and to devise what in later wars would be called "global" strategy. In fact, he was probably the only general on either side who could envision the war as a whole, the only one who was qualified to act as general-in-chief in a modern war. This is not the place to discuss his plan of grand operations for 1864, but it was a brilliant demonstration of strategic thinking and would do credit to the most finished student of a series of modern staff and command schools. Unhampered by traditional military doctrine Grant was boldly original in innovating new strategic concepts. A young officer once asked him what he thought of Jomini. Grant said he had never read the French-Swiss master, the guiding authority for so many other Civil War generals. He then expressed his own theory of war: "The art of war is simple enough. Find out where your enemy is. Get at him as soon as you can. Strike at him hard as you can, and keep moving on."

It is not true, however, as Grant stated in his memoirs and as many historians have repeated since, that Lincoln gave him an absolutely free hand in deciding strategy and directing operations. According to Grant's account, the President was a military innocent who greeted him with relief when he came to Washington and said, in effect: General, I am not a military man, I don't understand war and don't want to know your plans—go ahead and do exactly as you please. Grant wrote under the influence of his own postwar myth, which cast him in the image of the great soldier who was the architect of victory. Actually, as the evidence in contemporary war documents amply demonstrates, Lincoln, while permitting his general-in-chief wide latitude of action, watched him closely and never hesitated to check him when the need arose. On at least two occasions, as when he forced Grant to come to Washington to supervise personally the launching of the campaign against Jubal Early in the Shenandoah Valley and when he restrained him from removing General George H. Thomas before the battle of Nashville, he saved the general from serious mistakes.

Moreover, as the documents again show, the victorious strategy of the North was the joint product of consultations between Lincoln and Grant. The general submitted to Lincoln the broad outlines of his plans, and the President, approving the objectives and trusting Grant, did not seek to learn the details. Indeed, Grant made his strategy conform to the strategy Lincoln had been advocating since 1862: make enemy armies the objective and move all Federal forces against the enemy line simultaneously so as to bring into play the Federal advantage of superior numbers.

An offensive all along the line, violating the Jomini maxim of concentration, was the essence of Grant's strategy. When Grant explained to Lincoln this plan, so eminently sensible for the side with the greater numbers and the superior transportation, he remarked that those forces not fighting could still help the fighting by advancing. Grasping the point and recognizing the application of his own ideas, the President uttered a maxim of his own, one that for modern war was more valid than most of Jomini's dictums: "Those not skinning can hold a leg."

The 1864 command system was a major factor in the final victory of the North. By providing a sound basis for participation by the civil and military branches in the formulating of strategy, it gave the United States a modern command organization for a modern war. With a commander-in-chief to state policy and the general objectives of strategy, a general-in-chief to put the strategy in specific form, and a chief of staff to co-ordinate information, the United States possessed a model system of civil and military relationships and the finest command arrangements of any country in the world. Created in the strain of war, it expressed the national genius to improvise an arrangement to fit the requirements of the moment. The American system was superior to most command organizations then existing in Europe and was at least as good as the Prussian general staff machine. Indeed, it was probably the most efficient system that we have ever had.

The American Military System:
From Civil War To Global Conflict

I

AMERICANS ALWAYS turn quickly and eagerly from a war at its close and put its experience behind them. Perhaps this trait is to be explained by the outcome of our conflicts. Because we have never been defeated, we have not felt it necessary to examine critically the reasons for reverses or even the causes of victory. Satisfied with success, we have not looked for lessons in the past that might furnish guidance for the future. Practically all commentators on our military policy have stressed that we have blundered through our wars because in each conflict we repeat the errors of the preceding one, a view repeated so often that it has become axiomatic. But the converse would seem to be at least as true: we have blundered because we have not remembered or maintained the accomplishments of the preceding struggle.

The pattern of national behavior at the end of the Civil War was completely typical. The vast citizen armies that had been called into existence were demobilized, and the government returned to the practice of relying on a comparatively small regular army as the first line of land defense. The size of the army varied, expanding or contracting in response to the magnitude of Indian wars in the West or economy drives in Congress; it averaged 25,000 and was slightly larger in 1898 on the eve of the war with Spain. A second element in the land forces consisted of the voluntary militia units that by the time of the Civil War were coming to be known as the National Guard. The Militia Bill of 1792, which had left the training of the citizen soldiery to the states, had never, except in a few states, been enforced, with the result that by 1815 the militia had fallen into deserved disrepute and the original concept of the militia as a citizen army had almost disappeared. At the same time, however, in many states voluntary units emerged, existing in the militia system or side by side with it and supported by contributions from their commanders or members or by state aid. Whole companies and even regiments of these National Guards enlisted in the Mexican War and the Civil War. Although after 1865 there was an increasing unofficial co-operation between the National Guard and the regular army in such areas as training, the militia went pretty much its own way, and its units varied widely in quality of instruction and arms. Whatever shortcomings it possessed did not seem important, for in the minds of most national and state officials the principal function for which the militia existed was not to fight foreign enemies but to repress strikes and similar domestic disturbances. Congressman James A. Garfield, urging one general to draw up a plan for the organization of the militia based on the German Landwehr, declared that a more effective citizen army was needed to deal with "the dangers of communism."

Although the army was small and was sometimes treated by Congress as a military orphan, it was probably big enough to accomplish the policy objectives assigned to it. In the years of diplomatic isolation after 1865 the only enemies encountered by the United States were the Indians of the Western plains and mountains. From scattered posts all over the vast frontier area the army policed the red men and, when policing failed, fought them. The Indians were tough adversaries, and the army that finally broke them became in the process a tough little force, highly skilled in small-unit and individual tactics and endowed with a proud *ésprit de corps*. But the very techniques that the army had to develop to execute its mission had the result of afflicting the officers with a parochial viewpoint. Not only did the huge expanse of territory guarded by the troops require a dispersal of forces, but the nature of Indian warfare favored the employment of small units. Quite understandably, most officers came to have what might be called a post psychology. They felt heavily responsible for the detail of administration in their little commands, and they were rigidly aware that they must account for every detail to someone higher in the system. In an army phrase of the day, they became obsessed with the importance of "counting all the beans."

One of the best summaries of the army in this period was provided by Elihu Root, who later as Secretary of War would have a vital part in reforming its organization. He wrote:

Present utility was really the controlling consideration, and the possibility of war seemed at all times so vague and unreal that it had no formative power in shaping legislation regarding the army. The result was an elaborate system admirably adapted to secure pecuniary accountability and economy of expenditure in time of peace; a large number of small and separate commands, well officered and well disciplined, very efficient for police duty against Indians . . . ; and a class of officers most of whom were of a high order of individual excellence. . . . But the result did not include the effective organization and training of the army as a whole for the purpose of war.[1]

Nobody in high civil authority in the government seemed to think it alarming that the officer corps had no opportunity to study higher strategy or to gain experience in maneuvering larger bodies of troops. For that matter, nobody seemed to worry that the army was not organized "for the purpose of war." There was no apparent peril that called for the land forces to be organized on a war basis. In the minds of most national leaders and many military writers, the navy constituted the real first line of national defense and would meet any threat before it had a chance to reach our shores. While the army was held to a modest size after 1865, the navy experienced a sensational expansion. By 1898 the United States had the sixth largest navy in the world, and within a few years after 1900 it would advance to a top position among the ranking nautical powers.

The fine command system of 1864 that had been so instrumental in bringing victory to the North was scrapped after Appomattox, and army command arrangements at the highest level reverted to the system

[1] Elihu Root, *The Military and Colonial Policy of the United States* (Cambridge, Mass., 1916), 351–52.

in effect before 1860. The three principal elements were the Secretary of War, the commanding general, and the General Staff or bureau chiefs. During the war the chiefs, when they met as the Army Board, had functioned as a collective agency, but after 1865 they returned to their prewar character of individual administrators, each one pursuing his own objectives. As in the years preceding the war, the three segments of the system were also three contending forces for power. Their triple rivalry, with its sometimes incredible complexity, is difficult to describe. One way to summarize it is to say that the commanding general strove against the other two divisions, who strove back but who did not become allies because their causes of conflict with the general differed. The commanding general maneuvered to preserve his control of the line from the Secretary and sought to extend supervisory control over the staff. The bureau heads considered themselves responsible to the Secretary and denied the authority of the commanding general, but they accepted only a loose supervision from the Secretary. At times they acted as though they were subject only to the President and to Congress, where they had enormous lobbying influence.

The basic difficulty between the Secretary and the commanding general arose from a confusion of the functions of command with those of administration. In peace the duties of the general were almost entirely administrative. Having little to command, he tried to administer, on the theory he was commanding, and hence clashed with his civil superior at every turn. Because all orders and papers had to cross his desk, an ambitious commander could hamstring a weak

89

Secretary. On the other hand, a determined Secretary could drive a commander to distraction. (Jefferson Davis had had this effect on General Scott.) The commanding generals after 1865—Grant, W. T. Sherman, Philip Sheridan, John M. Schofield, and Nelson A. Miles—either bucked the system or sullenly adjusted to it. One, Sherman, became so disgusted that he removed his headquarters from Washington (as Scott had done after his clash with Davis).

Almost as irritating to the commanding general were his relations with the bureaus. It was not just that the chiefs defied his authority. The bureau officers had made their careers in Washington, and they had achieved what amounted to permanent tenure. The general, like other line officers, considered the chiefs bureaucrats who had put themselves out of touch with the line and with the needs of troops on line service. Curiously enough, the chiefs could have made the same criticism, in reverse, of the commander. Theoretically and usually in fact, the commanding general was the senior officer with the greatest reputation. Once appointed, he, like the chiefs, held office for the duration of his career. He knew as little about staff work as the staff did about line problems. Here was one of the gravest weaknesses in the command apparatus: there was no rotation of personnel between the administering and the fighting branches of the service.[2] It was a weakness that would become ominously apparent when the nation embarked on the

[2] Maj. Gen. Otto L. Nelson, *National Security and the General Staff* (Washington, 1946), 14–16; Walter Millis, *Arms and Men* (New York, 1956), 178–79.

industrial age of the twentieth century and the army entered the era of technological warfare.

In the post-Civil War period military education in the broad sense—education provided formally by schools or distilled through the writings of professional soldiers—was hardly on a par with that of the Mahan-Halleck renaissance. Only one important higher or postgraduate institution was added to the army's education system, the School of Application for Infantry and Cavalry, established in 1881 with the support of General Sherman at Fort Leavenworth, Kansas. More narrow and tactical in scope was a school of instruction for cavalry and light artillery set up at Fort Riley, Kansas, in 1892. Eventually the Leavenworth school would become the basic institution in the army's system of higher education, but at the moment, providing only a general survey of strategy and tactics, it was only a promising beginning. The same qualification must be made for the navy's small War College, which began operations in 1885.

From officers associated with the army schools came the few books on military subjects to appear in these years. In 1867 General Emory Upton, who taught at West Point and the Artillery School at Fort Monroe, published his *Infantry Tactics,* which was hailed as the greatest single advance in tactical instruction since the work of General Steuben during the Revolution. Heretofore, American authors of tactical manuals had borrowed their formations from the French, but Upton devised his largely from American experience. Colonel Arthur L. Wagner, who served on the

Leavenworth faculty for eleven years and left a deep imprint on the institution, produced two solid books that immediately became standard sources on their subjects: *The Service of Security and Information* (1893) and *Organization and Tactics* (1895).

These works were needed in the service, and wherever used they raised the professional competence of the officer corps. But they were almost entirely concerned with tactics rather than with strategy or policy. Upton, however, soon shifted his attention to larger aspects of war, and in so doing turned from the American to the European military experience. A brilliant and scholarly soldier, Upton was dispatched by the War Department to Europe and Asia to study the major armies of those areas. His report was published as a bulky book, *The Armies of Asia and Europe* (1878). Then Upton began to research and write what he envisioned as his great work, *The Military Policy of the United States from 1775*. He had completed the narrative down to the middle of the Civil War at the time of his death in 1881. The book was not published, but Upton transmitted the manuscript to Sherman, then commanding general, and Sherman and other high officers read it. Thus Upton's ideas were fairly well known to the army before and after his death. But the book would have its greatest influence when Secretary Root discovered the manuscript and made its teachings the foundation of many of his great army reforms.[3]

---

[3] It was Root who caused the book to be published: Emory Upton, *The Military Policy of the United States from 1775* (Washington, 1904). There were four subsequent reprintings.

Upton's announced purpose was to expose what he called the "folly and criminality" of American military policy. His thesis is widely familiar, if for no other reason than that it has colored nearly all later writing of military history. The United States had blundered into every war unprepared, Upton contended, and had struggled through each conflict at immense and needless cost. Although Upton buttressed his conclusions with the apparatus of historical scholarship, the indictment simply was not supported by the evidence of history. It was certainly not true of the Mexican War, and it was not true of the Civil War after the North had shifted to a war basis. To prevent a repetition of the debacles he saw in the past, Upton recommended the creation of a compact professional army that could be expanded quickly in event of war. This concept of the "expansible army" was an old and favorite one with regular army officers. It had been put forward by the generals after the War of 1812 and had been advocated by Secretary Calhoun, and it was probably from Calhoun's reports that Upton got the idea. Again Upton was misreading history, and, strangely enough, history of which he had been a part. The Civil War had not been fought by professional armies but by citizen-soldiers, and Upton had led such men and should have known their worth. Upton's proposal of a large professional army was not acceptable to his generation. But in arguing that the nation must have a land force big enough to accomplish any possible policy objective he was anticipating the future. This was the same doctrine of adequate preparedness that

Alfred Thayer Mahan would shortly preach for the navy and that would ultimately seem so seductive to the American people.

Less familiar to the public than his views on military policy, but having a profound impact on the officer corps, were Upton's ideas about American command arrangements. He did not carry his study of the Civil War far enough to consider the 1864 system but concentrated his attention on events in 1862 when Lincoln was trying to make McClellan fight. Upton's interpretation of what had happened was characteristically misleading. Working largely from pro-McClellan sources, he concluded that the general was the victim of political interference by Lincoln and Secretary of War Stanton. But while he did not absolve Lincoln, Upton put the major blame on Stanton. In his account, the imperious Stanton dominated Lincoln, seized control of the war machine, and sabotaged McClellan. The picture could hardly be more false. We do not have as yet an adequate biography of Stanton and hence cannot assess his true role in the war, but whatever his position we know that he did not control Lincoln. Rather, the reverse was true: in all important matters Stanton acted as the President's deputy. But Upton had a motive in exaggerating Stanton's influence. He wanted to demonstrate, as he admitted, the fault of a system which in his day still permitted the "Secretary of War to usurp military command." Upton had a remedy for this situation. Highly impressed by the Germans, he proposed the creation of a general staff system. Previous American military writers had advocated our borrowing European strategical and tactical concepts, but none had gone so far as to suggest we adopt a European command pattern. Upton was saying, in effect, that for the purpose of modern war the American military experience was useless. In making his case he perpetrated some historical errors that would affect the thinking of later military men and that would survive in the history books up into our own time.

2

Upton's picture of an America blundering into conflict unprepared was true at least of the war with Spain. There has never been a war quite like the struggle of 1898. As the newspaper humorist "Mr. Dooley" put it, the United States fought the war in a dream, but Spain, fortunately, was in a trance. It was the last small, individualistic war before the huge, impersonal contests of the twentieth century. Begun in April, it was over by August, and the most important land fighting, in Cuba, lasted only a month. Enthusiastically reported by the press (89 reporters accompanied the army of 17,000 to Cuba), it produced enough heroes and slogans to stock half a dozen larger wars. It offered such features as an assistant Secretary of the Navy (Theodore Roosevelt) determining a vital strategic objective—to attack the Philippines—when his superior was absent from the office; the winning of a great naval battle (Manila) with only one American casualty, a man who died of heat stroke; and a 300-pound general (William R. Shafter) leading in tropical Cuba an army clad in woolen uniforms. Despite its comic aspects, however, the war had immense effects. It transformed the United States into a colonial and a world power and thus made almost inevitable American participation in the world wars of the next century.

At the outbreak of hostilities the regular army of 28,000 was prepared for anything except large-scale war. There had been no brigade formation of troops in the country for thirty years, and only a few of the officers had seen as large a unit as a regiment assembled in one place. Obviously a larger force would be required to deal with Spain, and Congress authorized the President to increase the army to 62,000 and to call for 125,000 volunteers. It was expected that the National Guard would furnish the bulk of the volunteers, and many militia regiments did offer their services. But the state troops were, except for a knowledge of close-order drill, virtually untrained, and they were armed, if at all, with the old single-shot Springfield rifles that fired a black-powder cartridge. In short, the United States, about to fight its first foreign war since 1846, had to mobilize what amounted to a new army—and to do this without a previously prepared plan of mobilization or any program for assembling and handling a large body of troops.

Over 200,000 men were brought into service in the space of a few months. The effort of the War Department to train them and to transport them overseas resulted in a complete shambles. The supply departments had on hand enough weapons, clothing, and other matériel for the existing army and a slight surplus. They were unable during the war to increase substantially some of the items in short supply. For example, the regulars were equipped with the new Krag-Jorgensen repeating rifles, but there were never enough of these pieces to arm the volunteers. The bureau chiefs were not entirely to be blamed for the procurement failures. They were asked to do a big job without warning, and they labored with inadequate staffs (there were only 57 officers in the entire Quartermaster Department). But basically the trouble was not procurement but distribution. In most cases the supplies were available, but the staff agencies could not put them where they were needed. The confusion at Port Tampa, Florida, where the regulars were assembled, was almost incredible. A typical scene was reported by General Nelson A. Miles:

To illustrate . . . present conditions, fifteen cars loaded with uniforms were side-tracked twenty-five miles away from Tampa, and remained there for weeks while the troops suffered for clothing. Five thousand rifles, which were discovered yesterday, were needed by several regiments. Also the different parts of the siege train and ammunition for same . . . are scattered through hundreds of cars on the side-tracks of the railroad.

One army critic, in trying to describe the inefficiency of the bureaus, could say only: "The staff departments failed to pull together. . . . In a thousand ways there was lack of coordination which not only led to miscarriage of plans but to extravagance in expenditures and lack of harmony in administration." The Dodge Commission, investigating the conduct of the war, was more restrained in its condemnation of the War Department and of most of the bureaus. But the very understatement of its official language carried a special bite: ". . . there was lacking in the general administration of the War Department . . . that complete grasp of the situation which was essential to the highest efficiency and discipline of the Army."

When the facts became known at the close of hostilities, it was the breakdown in the mobilization and training process that most outraged public opinion. Critics of the War Department's performance paid little attention to any deficiencies exhibited in the high command arrangements or in the strategic direction of the war. And yet in these areas there had been shortcomings and failures almost as grave as those in supply. No over-all plan of operations had been worked out before the war, mainly and simply because no agency in the military establishment was charged with the function of preparing strategy. Secretary of War Russell A. Alger, an amiable politician but a most incompetent administrator, at first turned for counsel—he soon learned better—to Nelson A. Miles, the commanding general, who as a young officer had led a division in the Civil War and had later won fame as an Indian fighter. But now, older and in a foreign war, Miles seemed out of his element. He vacillated between places where the troops should be assembled, between the training programs they should receive, and between the overseas objectives the army should strike, Puerto Rico or Cuba. As Secretary Alger feelingly commented: "Many of the general's proposals were obviously impracticable, and not infrequently absolutely impossible." Santiago, Cuba, was finally selected as the main objective, merely because the public was demanding action and the known presence of the Spanish fleet at that place indicated the enemy might fight to hold it.

Alger, Miles, and their naval counterparts had, of course, to frame and execute strategy under the authority of the commander-in-chief, President William McKinley, who did not forget that he had seen service in the Civil War as a major. McKinley, in the tradition of Polk and Lincoln, assumed active command of the land and sea forces. He set up a headquarters post in his office, adorned with wall maps marked by pins, from whence he kept in telegraphic touch with operations in all theaters. Almost daily he presided over general strategy discussions with the Secretary of War, the Secretary of the Navy, and the bureau chiefs. Although the President seemed to have his finger on every detail, often revising orders and not hesitating to instruct commanders in the field, his control was more apparent than actual. Basically, McKinley was a manager rather than a director of men. As President he restored to the office some of the prestige it had lost since 1865, not by confronting Congress with a show of power but by cajoling and persuading its members. As commander-in-chief he tended to evade exercising his authority in a conflict of views. Thus when called on to decide if the army and navy should jointly attack Santiago, a matter that only he could decide, he replied: "General Shafter and Admiral Sampson should confer at once for cooperation in taking Santiago. After the fullest exchange of views they should determine the time and manner of attack." If Alger was no Stanton and Miles no Grant, McKinley was certainly no Lincoln.

3

One man was aware of the planlessness that had characterized the entire conduct of operations. This was Elihu Root, who in 1899 was appointed Secretary of War by McKinley. Root was a great public servant who made his mark in two cabinet offices, War and State. Probably it was in the former office that he made his most enduring contribution to national development. He took over the War Department at a time when revelations of inefficiency in the late conflict were reverberating through the country, threatening, it seemed, to destroy public confidence in the whole military establishment. His mission, as assigned by the President, was to recommend reforms in organization that would avert a repetition of the debacle of 1898 and place the army on a modern basis. A patient investigator, Root read the voluminous report of the Dodge Commission, and he talked to officers who could give him firsthand accounts of what had gone wrong in the campaigns against the Spanish. The thing that shocked him above all was the lack of co-ordination in nearly every aspect of the war. This, he concluded, was because no agency in the army was charged with supervising the execution of "detailed plans made beforehand."

Impressed by the inadequacies of the existing system, Root did not push his inquiries back to see whether anything better had existed in the past. Instead he turned to studying the command arrangements of European countries. He interviewed officers who were familiar with the general staff systems of Germany and France. He read the works of the British military writer Spenser Wilkinson, who greatly admired the German system. And finally he found the books of Upton and then the manuscript of the general's *Military Policy*, which Root caused to be published at government expense. Upton's writings became Root's principal source of ideas and his chief reliance. Root acknowledged that "they gave me the details on which I could base recommendations and overcome my ignorance as a civilian."

Root found Upton's writings so attractive because they confirmed what had come to be a basic conviction with the Secretary, namely, that the American military experience offered little if any guidance for the future. Although Root was always careful to pay tribute to the men of the past, he was a little patronizing in his remarks, and he obviously accepted the Uptonian axiom that we had blundered through every war. We had won the wars, or at least had not lost them, Root had to concede, because the American people were remarkably adept at getting up "a jury-rigged, extempore organization . . . adapted to the circumstances." But in future wars we could not depend, as heretofore, on American character rising "superior to system, or rather absence of system." We should have a definite and detailed system worked out beforehand, Root contended, and in devising it we should take due note of the experience of European nations:

Neither our political nor our military system makes it suitable that we should have a general staff organized like the German general staff or the French general staff; but the common experience of mankind is that the things which those general staffs do have to be done in every well managed and well directed army, and they have to be done by a body of men especially assigned to do them. We should have such a body of men selected and organized in our own way and in accordance with our own system to do those essential things.[4]

An American variation of a European system, then, was what Root wanted, and while he and his advisers studied the organizations of various nations they were obviously most impressed by the general staff system of Germany. It is not surprising that the American planners should turn to the Germans for a model. Germany's victories over France and Austria had made her the leading power in Europe, and her command arrangements were believed to be the secret of her success. The system that Root would establish resembled closely in structure the German design, and it cannot be understood without reference to its prototype. At the head of the German system was the Great General Staff, which was presided over by a chief of staff who was the adviser of the commander-in-chief, the emperor. But the Great General Staff was not the only important unit in the

[4] Root, *The Military and Colonial Policy of the United States,* 422–23.

system. There was a military cabinet that was responsible for personnel and a war ministry that was responsible for organization and supply. The Great General Staff was in time of peace completely a planning organization—planning for war. It was not burdened with daily administrative detail or supervision of bureaus. The staff officers worked out plans of mobilization, studied advances in ordnance and tactics, prepared maps of areas where the army might have to fight, participated in war games on maps in their offices or on maneuvers with troops in the field, and, most important, considered and drew up plans for every possible war which the government might decide to undertake.

The Great General Staff has been aptly described as a brain, planning in peace for war. Not until war came did it spring into action and not until then did it become the commanding agency of the army, at which time it took over the direction of operations. In short, it was a body of limited functions—in peace it planned and in war it became the combat command. It was not an organ of control over the entire army. One more feature of the German system remains to be described. The Germans frequently put royalty, the emperor or a royal prince, in titular command of their army. But as the contemporary Hohenzollerns were not noticeably bright in military matters, the actual command had to be exercised by somebody else, and the obvious choice was the chief of staff. Thus this officer planned strategy before a war and then directed operations after war broke. The elder Moltke in the Franco-Prussian War was both chief of staff and general-in-chief.

Root's ideas for the new army—the Root reforms, as they came to be called—were put into effect by Congressional authorization and executive action between 1900 and 1903. Before examining the program, it is necessary to understand the Secretary's objectives as he announced them, although he himself was not as clear on some of them as he thought he was. His basic assumption, voiced over and over, was that the only purpose in having an army was to provide for war. Nobody would deny such a trite statement, Root said, but the American army had been administered on a contrary and erroneous theory—"present utility," economy and convenience of accountability, had been the controlling consideration. A system founded on present utility could not stand the test of modern war, could not supply the co-ordination of effort in every part of the machine that modern war demanded. To achieve this co-ordination, Root proposed the creation of a general staff, one of whose functions would be to study strategy and formulate war plans before wars. As part of his plan, he was determined to abolish what he considered the anomalous office of General-in-Chief, thereby eliminating the constant administrative friction between the holder of that post and the Secretary.

The Root program may be best seen if the whole is presented in summary form. The principal parts were as follows:

1. An enlarged regular army. Congress authorized a force with a minimum size of 60,000 and a maximum of 100,000.

2. Federal supervision, of a very loose nature, of the National Guard, provided in the Dick Act of 1903.

3. Organization of an elaborate system of education, consisting of a number of service schools and crowned by the Army Staff College and the Army War College. More and better facilities were necessary to instruct the additional officers required in the expanded army; of 1,118 newly commissioned officers only 276 were graduates of West Point.

4. Interchangeable service of staff and line officers, with permanent staff assignments being ended and all staff officers returning to the line after staff tenure.

5. Establishment of a general staff headed by a Chief of Staff, to whom the bureau heads, the old General Staff officers, would report.

Congressional legislation of 1903 authorizing the creation of the general staff abolished the office of General-in-Chief, and its last holder, General Miles, took his departure, not very graciously, and the first Chief of Staff, S. M. B. Young, appeared.

The most important part of the new system—indeed, its very heart—was the general staff arrangement, the device that was to oversee the entire establishment. From the viewpoint of command the vital elements in the system were the Chief of Staff and the War Department general staff. The latter agency consisted of a group of officers divided into sections, each of which performed a specific function; collectively these officers were to advise the Chief of Staff on broad matters of policy. The Chief of Staff was the immediate adviser of the Secretary, who was the deputy executive of the President. All orders emanating from the Chief of Staff were issued in the Secretary's name. Root was always careful to emphasize that his system insured civilian control of the military arm, "civilian control to be exercised through a single military expert of high rank, who is provided with an adequate corps of professional assistants . . ."

At first glance the American staff system seemed to be an exact duplicate of the German system, from which it presumably had drawn its inspiration. Both organizations were headed by a Chief of Staff, and the War Department general staff was obviously intended to be the American equivalent of the Great General Staff. But the similarities were largely structural; the two systems differed in significant detail. Unlike his German counterpart, the American Chief of Staff could not take the field in war as general-in-chief. He would have to remain in Washington to execute the functions assigned to his agency. Our general staff—in contrast to the purely planning function of its German counterpart—was charged with a multitude of administrative duties, the most important of which was the supervision of the bureau chiefs. Two enigmatic but enormously elastic words spelled the greatest deviation between the American and German systems. The Chief of Staff was to "supervise" the entire military establishment, and the general staff was to "co-ordinate" the establishment. "This was no minor change of concept; this was no mere adaptation to American institutions," says Alvin Brown, a severe critic of the Root program. "It was a reconstruction of the most fundamental nature. It amounted to an entirely different sort of agency." [5]

The derivation of the Root staff concept is not clear. It may be, as General John M. Palmer has sug-

[5] Alvin Brown, *The Armor of Organization* (New York, 1953), 214.

gested, that when the German *Generalstab* was translated into English as "general staff" it conveyed a
meaning quite different from that of the original.
The English phrase implied an agency with a general
or supervisory relation to the military establishment,
whereas the true English equivalent of *Generalstab*
would have been the generalship staff or the strategic
staff.[6] It could be that Root borrowed the notion of
staff supervision from the French system, although
the French believed that in event of war the Chief of
Staff should take command in the field, on the theory
that the man who was to use the instrument in war
should shape and sharpen it in peace. Or Root may
have taken the idea of co-ordination from the practice of the business world he knew so well. At the
turn of the century "co-ordinate" was becoming a
popular word with business experts and was on the
way to the almost sacred position it has since attained
in the administration of American government, cor-
porations, and universities.

Of course, it is possible that Root did not realize
fully all the implications of the supervisory function
or understand exactly how his system would work in
all situations. When the general staff bill was presented
to Congress, it was scrutinized closely by the Senate
Military Affairs Committee, all of whose members
were veterans of the Civil War. These men wanted
to change the term "supervise" to "command" or
"control." Root successfully resisted the alteration,
but his explanation of the role of the general staff was
hardly precise: "Those are the two great duties of

[6] John McAuley Palmer, *America in Arms* (New Haven,
1941), 125.

the General Staff—first, to acquire information and
to arrange it and fit it into all the possible plans of
operation, so that an order can be intelligently made,
and second, when the order has been made, to exercise constant supervision that does not mean command but to inform and advise the different persons
who must conspire to the execution of the order of
how every other one is going on with his work."
Whatever Root's motives and objectives, it is evident
that his system differed not only from contemporary
European systems but departed from the practice of
the American past.

There is another possible explanation for the Root
concept of staff function. The Secretary was obsessed
with the idea that the office of General-in-Chief must
be eliminated. He contended that in time of peace
no officer could exercise the power of commanding
general. Law required the Secretary to supervise the
expenditure of money for military purposes, and
since every important activity of the army required
the use of money, the Secretary had to control the
peacetime operations of the army. What he seemed to
be saying was that in peace there could be no commander except the Secretary, who would act through
the medium of the Chief of Staff, who would have
supervisory but not command powers and hence
could not conflict with his civil superior. While Root
was right in thinking that the Secretary and the
general-in-chief could not both represent the President in command of the army or divide the command between them, apparently it did not occur to
him that the commanding general could act as the
Secretary's deputy in the same way that the Secretary

acted as the President's deputy. Nor did Root see that, although the Chief of Staff was to function in an advisory capacity, actually that officer, because everything cleared through his office and because his technical knowledge was much greater than that of the civilian Secretary, would exercise considerable command authority.

In all of Root's arguments detailing the advantages of having a chief of staff instead of a commanding general, the Secretary seemed to be thinking only of peacetime conditions. When he said that experience had shown that it was impossible for any officer to act as general-in-chief in peace, he implied that it would be possible in war. Conversely, when he said that the Secretary's position required him to control all the operations of the army in peace, he implied that it would not be required in war. Root never explained why one set of standards was imperative in peace and would not be imperative in war. The unresolved question was this: if in time of war it became necessary to appoint a general-in-chief in command of all field forces, what would be the command relation between him and the Chief of Staff? Would the general frame his own strategy, or would he act within a strategic framework devised by the Chief of Staff and his professional assistants? [7] Possibly Root did not face up to this issue because he had not carried

[7] There is a question of terminology here that cannot be completely resolved. It would be possible, of course, to have in war several field or theater commanders who would be subordinate to the Chief of Staff. But apparently Root was thinking in terms of one commander of all field forces, a general-in-chief in the style of Grant in the Civil War.

his thinking beyond peacetime conditions. Or he may have been so influenced by Upton's description of the baleful role of Stanton that he did not believe the Secretary, or his deputy, the Chief of Staff, should control in war. As for the first Chiefs of Staff, they were either confused by their status or they resented it. The anomalous position of the Chief was the greatest weakness in the system, said Hugh L. Scott when he retired from the office: "This power, this right to command in the Secretary's name, which in the French and German armies is so clearly expressed and fully acceded to, is implied in phrases such as 'coordinating functions,' 'supervisory capacity,' etc., but there has existed and there still seems to exist, a shirking from saying quite boldly that, under the Secretary of War, the Chief of Staff commands the Army. . . ."

After Root's lustrous description of how a staff system functioned, the actual work of the general staff in the years following its creation seemed highly anticlimactic. The agency at the head of the system, the War Department general staff, consisted of three divisions; the third of these, "military education and technical matters," handled planning. The division's idea of planning was to assign officers studying at the Army War College to write monographs on subjects selected by staff officers who wanted a particular subject investigated. The results were interesting. A great amount of research was done, and a large number of scholarly studies were turned out. Invariably the monographs contained a good deal of useful information, but hardly ever were they concerned with war in its higher aspects. Root proudly described these projects to Congress as though they represented the large purpose for which the general staff was created, but in reality the list dealt with matters of administrative routine. The very volume of this busywork suggests that the Secretary and the staff were primarily concerned with justifying the existence of the new system to Congress.

When Leonard Wood became Chief of Staff in 1910, he was astounded to discover the immense amount of paper work occupying the organization. He and another officer picked out at random one hundred studies submitted to his office and decided that not one related to war and that only three were of any general consequence. At Wood's instigation the general staff was reorganized into four divisions, with the War College section assuming the function of planning. The new agency avoided the haphazard methods of the previous third division, concentrating upon the framing of a detailed military policy and an appraisal of the militia. This was an improvement on what had gone before, but the general staff was still not performing the function for which supposedly it existed: to prepare plans for every possible demand that national policy might make of the military. When the planners discussed a military policy for the United States, they thought entirely in terms of a policy for peacetime; when they discussed war plans, they thought only in terms of a defensive war. But they could hardly have thought in any other terms. National policy was vaguely discernible after 1900—it pointed in the direction of greater involvement in world politics—but it had never been sharply defined. Indeed, because of its implications, it could not be defined. The political directors of policy could not afford to admit, perhaps could not bring themselves to believe, that the United States might have to fight a foreign war. Nor could the war planners prepare for a war not envisaged in national policy.

The defensive orientation of military thought was apparent in the attempts made to bring the army and navy together for joint strategic consultations. Naval reorganization after the war with Spain resembled developments in the army, coming as a result of much the same kind of agitation without following exactly the same lines. In 1900 a General Board of officers was created to advise the Secretary of the Navy concerning the demands that national policy might make on the navy and to prepare war plans.[8] With the general staff idea taking shape in the Navy Department, Root envisioned a joint high level agency to co-ordinate interservice planning, and at his urging the Joint Army and Navy Board was established by letter authority of the two Secretaries. Presumably this agency was to consider the highest aspects of national strategy and ways to combine the striking force of both services in war. The Board did consider the problem of American interests in the Pacific and drew up a series of plans to meet any enemy in that area. But much of

[8] The functions of the General Board were completely advisory, and it had no supervisory relation to the whole naval establishment. The line of command ran down from the Secretary to the bureaus. The navy bureau chiefs were even more strongly intrenched than their army counterparts and registered co-ordination more successfully. Not until 1915 did Congress authorize the creation of an office similar to the Chief of Staff, the Chief of Naval Operations, and this functionary was not provided with a corps of staff assistants.

the time the Board occupied itself with studies of coastal and lake defenses and produced much the same kind of informative but abstract reports as emanated from the general staff.

But it would be unfair to judge the general staff mechanism solely by its performance in the salad years of its existence. If Root was not completely aware of all the implications of the system he had created, other people and elements in the organization were more confused, and some were flatly hostile to the new arrangement. Few if any officers appreciated the true function of a general staff officer—to act as a professional expert—and no members of the corps had been educated for general staff work. In short, here was a general staff system that began operations without any general staff officers. Eventually the service and staff schools would produce specialists of all kinds—they were, in fact, producing specialists at the division and corps level by the time of our entrance into World War I—but it was not until 1935 that a graduate of Root's educational system became Chief of Staff. Many of the older officers resented the trained younger officers coming out of the Army Staff College, the so-called "Leavenworth clique," and fought them at every turn. Especially resentful were the bureau chiefs, who disliked the pretensions of the staff officers and resisted the attempts of the general staff to exercise supervisory control over them. Command relations between the Chief of Staff and the bureau had not been resolved by the outbreak of World War I. "In spite of the real advance in control following the creation of the General Staff . . . ," writes F. L. Paxson, "no satis-

factory balance had ever been established between the
General Staff as adviser of the Secretary of War and
the permanent bureaus of the War Department
through which the peace Army was actually gov-
erned, fed, clothed, and armed. There was a perpetual
feud between the Chief of Staff and the Adjutant
General, and competition among the several supply
bureaus . . . , each of which bought for itself." [9]

Bureau influence was partially responsible for keeping the general staff at a small size. Originally the
agency had 45 officers, but in 1912 the number was
cut to 36. As part of the defense program inaugurated
after World War I began, Congress allowed an increase of 18, but these were to come in five annual
increments. When the United States entered the war
in 1917, there were only 9 officers in Washington to
supervise and co-ordinate the whole establishment
and 11 in the War College Division to prepare war
plans (22 were stationed elsewhere). By contrast, the
staff systems of Germany, France, and England numbered, respectively, 650, 644, and 232. But it would
be unfair to lay on the bureaus all the blame for the
inadequate size of the staff, as unfair as to blame the
staff for all the inadequacies of its performance.
The plain truth is that nobody—the government, the
people, the general staff itself—seriously believed that
the United States might ever be involved in a great
war. The staff planners, working on their projects to
repel a hypothetical invader, were but reflecting the
military mores of society. Despite all Root's reforms,

[9] Frederic L. Paxson, *America at War, 1917–1918* (Boston,
1939), 35.

"present utility" was still a controlling consideration in the system.[10]

Still, on the eve of American entrance into World War I, the military organization clearly was in almost every way a more efficient body than it had been at the beginning of the century. The changes which had been inaugurated since the war with Spain had resulted in an improved officer corps, a greater professional competence in both staff and line, and a more effective co-ordination at some of the higher levels of command. But it was not clear that the system created by Root was capable of successfully waging a major war. The general staff had not before the war come to grips with the immense problems of modern war, and it was not permitted to prepare for the global conflict it would be called on to conduct. President Wilson seemed to think there was no relation between foreign and military policy. According to General Bliss, when the President read in a newspaper that the general staff was readying a plan for a possible war with Germany, he went "white with passion" and threatened to order every staff officer out of Washington. Later Secretary of War Newton D.

[10] It is a common American practice to meet a situation by passing a law or creating an organization to deal with it. The assumption is that if some kind of institutional action is taken the particular problem has been taken care of and need cause no more worry. Thus the passage of the Sherman Antitrust Act supposedly settled the problem of big business. The early history of the general staff suggests that the American people may think in a similar fashion about military matters. An organization to handle these matters had been created—so all the problems of war could be forgotten.

Baker tried to explain to Wilson that the staff planners made war with every country in the world as a paper exercise and that this was part of their job. The commander-in-chief replied: "That seems to me a very dangerous occupation. I think you had better stop it." Perhaps the gravest defect in the system was the question that Root had left unresolved—the command status of the Chief of Staff. Would that officer by virtue of his supervisory authority direct operations in the field? Or would the strategic direction of the field forces rest with a general-in-chief? The Root system, which was an adaptation of European practices without incorporating European command concepts and which ignored the best of the American military experience, was about to receive a severe test.

4

The United States had never been in a war like the one it entered in 1917. It was a global conflict that pitted one coalition of nations against another. Much more so than the Civil War, it was a war of matériel, calling for the expenditure of vast amounts of supplies and demanding the organization of the whole resources of the nation for military purposes. And more than the Civil War, it was total in its impact upon society, compelling the government to mobilize men, money, matériel, and even opinion. It required of the United States an infinitely greater war effort than any struggle in the past. An army of three and a half million men was assembled, and over two million of this force was transported overseas to the fighting front in France. The economy was geared to war objectives and, under the direction of the War Industries Board and other agencies—agencies that illustrate perfectly the enlarged role of the civilian in modern war, performed enormous productive feats. Because the war was modern and total and global, command arrangements were correspondingly more intricate and involved than in previous and less complex conflicts. It is not surprising that the men in the top positions in the American military system did not understand all the implications and requirements of command in this new kind of war. But it is a matter of some surprise that they could not relate their problems to the nexus of history. They knew almost nothing of American command experiences in the past, and what little they did know was usually wrong. Heading the list of the uninformed was the commander-in-chief, that former eminent historian, Dr. Woodrow Wilson.

In Wilson's *History of the American People,* the volume dealing with the Civil War was remarkable for the unrealistic way in which strategy was treated. The author did, indeed, describe the great strategic movements of the war, in some detail and in rather vivid language, but he never told who planned the movements or why particular movements were decided upon. A reader might well have got the impression that the strategy was the product of cosmic forces. Wilson, who had studied so closely the evolu-

117

tion of parliamentary systems, either did not understand the importance of command systems or was not interested in the subject. It was probably the latter. As commander-in-chief, he was no Polk or Lincoln, not even a McKinley. He did not set up a command post in the White House, he did not follow feverishly the course of the fighting, he did not supervise the appointments of commanders. These things and even the direction of industrial mobilization he left almost entirely to Secretary of War Newton D. Baker.

Baker, a former lawyer and Progressive politician, proved to be an able administrator who could grasp the reins of the vast war machine that was called into existence. But Baker's knowledge of military history was largely limited to what his father, a Confederate cavalryman, had related to him about the Civil War. According to the father's version—and Baker testified that it left an abiding impression on him—the South had the better of the war for so long because President Davis let his generals alone, while Lincoln and Stanton interfered constantly with theirs. This, of course, was the familiar and false picture that Upton and other military men had helped to popularize. Actually, as we have seen, Davis interfered frequently with military affairs, generally with unfortunate results; Lincoln interfered just as often, but most of his interventions were intelligent and salutary. To Baker, however, the lesson of the Civil War was that civilians should not interfere with generals. Eventually he would modify his command concepts, but he assumed office in a modern war with the unmodern idea that strategy was something narrowly military and to be determined exclusively by military men.

The third important figure in the command apparatus was the man selected to command the army in France, the American Expeditionary Force—John J. Pershing. Pershing was a driving and decisive personality who was sensitively aware of his responsibilities as field commander, and of his rights as general-in-chief. He saw, as did Baker also, that the strategic possibilities open to the United States were limited. There was no choice either of theater of operations or line of communications. The war was in France, and the job of this country was to bring her strength to bear there in co-operation with her allies as quickly as possible. To Pershing, therefore, the chief function of the War Department was to serve his every need, to furnish him with everything he called for. He organized in France a headquarters staff that not only advised with him on strategic matters but controlled all the services of supply in the zone of war. So intent was Pershing on the immediate task at hand that he even objected to the promotion of staff officers assigned to duties in Washington.

Both during and after the war Pershing was bitterly critical of the general staff for failing to meet his constant demands for supplies. His chief complaint was that he did not receive needed matériel in the amount he requested, while often getting an excess of items he did not need. On one occasion he angrily cabled Washington that the War Department must send him exactly what he asked for and not matériel that happened to be on hand or that some staff officer thought the army should have. Pershing's strictures should have been directed at the bureau chiefs. Many of these officers were old men, near the retiring age, and the habits of long years of peacetime routine were strong upon them. They could not expand their thinking on procurement to the devouring demands of modern war. Under the strain of supplying the army in France the bureaus broke down, and it is hardly an exaggeration to say that at one stage the entire war effort approached catastrophe.

The crisis was met by assigning to the general staff the job of supervising the work of the bureaus. Almost continuously since the beginning of the war the general staff had been going through a progressive reorganization as it sought to put itself on a footing where it could cope with the problems of the war, and it was one of the new divisions that had emerged, Storage and Traffic, that took over supervision of the bureaus. This agency performed its task with reasonable competence, but only at the expense of assuming a heavy administrative burden. So closely did it supervise the bureaus that it became almost an operative supply service.

In Pershing's concept of his command position one consideration overshadowed all others. He was the general-in-chief, and he commanded directly under the President and the Secretary of War. No military person or power must be interposed between the President and his commander; the line of authority must run from the highest in the land to the highest in the field. Obviously Pershing thought of himself as holding a position similar to Grant's. In fact, in the general's entourage it was common talk to liken Grant's and Pershing's command roles. General James G. Harbord, chief of staff of the AEF, defending Pershing's determination to command under the President, said that no successful war had ever been fought by a staff officer in a distant capital. As an example of attempted staff interference Harbord cited the 1864 command system: "Henry W. Halleck tried unsuccessfully to interpose himself between President Lincoln and Lieutenant General Grant." Here again was a case of military men misunderstanding military history. Halleck as Chief of Staff had had no power to command, not even to co-ordinate, and he had not tried to interpose between Lincoln and Grant. But to the Pershing circle Halleck was too good a historical illustration to overlook. They could use Lincoln's Chief of Staff to oppose the command claims of the Chief of Staff of the Root system.

At the beginning of the war the Chief of Staff was Hugh Scott, who soon retired and was succeeded by Tasker Bliss. So lightly regarded, apparently, was the position that Bliss was detached for service abroad, and for a period in 1918 the office was administered by an acting chief until Pershing, at the urging of Baker, sent Peyton C. March from France to occupy it. March was the fourth key figure in the command system. A dedicated and deeply learned soldier, March was as determined as Pershing to subordinate everything to the winning of the war. And, like Pershing, he was fully aware of the rights and powers of the position he held. His authority was defined by Secretary Baker, who had become convinced of the importance of the Chief of Staff's role. By the terms of War Department orders, the Chief of Staff took "rank and precedence" over all officers of the army. He was charged with the "planning, development, and execution" of the army program. In the name of the Secretary he issued such orders as were necessary to insure that the "policies" of the War Department were "harmoniously executed." To March this Rootian language was clear enough. The Chief of Staff ranked and was superior to the general-in-chief. Pershing was a subordinate, to be upheld "as long as we kept him in command in France." Baker, the Secretary who had originally thought that civilian interference with a field commander was dangerous, was now willing to "supervise" the commander through the medium of a military deputy. To Pershing, of course, supervision meant command, and he was determined to resist it. The inevitable result was continuous controversy between March and Pershing.

One episode will illustrate the nature of the clash engendered by the March and Pershing concepts of command. In July, 1918, somebody, probably March, persuaded Baker that Pershing should have more time to devote to "military" tasks. As Baker told Pershing, the people thought of him as their "fighting general," and the War Department wanted to strengthen this impression. It was thought that Pershing's labors could be eased—and his reputation enhanced—by the curious device of dividing his authority. The War Department contemplated sending to France a general staff officer to take charge of the services of supply. This officer would control the flow of supplies from the United States to the zone of the army and would have co-ordinate authority with Pershing. Pershing's angry protest blocked this proposal. "Please let us not make the mistake of handicapping our army here by attempting to control these things from Washington, or by introducing any co-ordinate authority," he cabled. "The whole must remain absolutely under one head. . . . The man who fights the armies must control their supplies through subordinates responsible to him alone."

Of this and other attempts by Pershing to resist supervision by the general staff, March wrote: "As the AEF increased in size, General Pershing's inability to function in teamwork with his legal and authorized superiors increased. . . . He wanted a rubber stamp for Chief of Staff at home, so he could be entirely independent of any supervision or control." In part, the clash between March and Pershing can be written off as the inevitable irritation that would occur in any organization when two strong men are placed in conjunction. But it was more than that. The conflict was inherent in the system created by Root. That system had raised the technical and professional excellence of the army to new levels, but in its aping of European models and its ambiguous allocation of powers it had forgotten too much of the American command experience. The "jury-rigged, extemporized" agencies of the past that Root scorned had sprung, after all, from the popular genius and the requirements of the American scene. Indeed, it was precisely such extemporized arrangements that made the Root system work in the war. From the command record of the war some critics have concluded that the general staff failed in the event for which it was created and that, therefore, the whole staff concept was basically wrong. A more objective judgment would seem to be that the concept was sound enough, but the machinery to execute it needed to be improved. The Root system was an adaptation of European arrangements that did not incorporate the best European practices. Nor did it represent the best experience of the American military past. More of that experience would have to be infused into the system borrowed from Europe before the general staff would be able to cope with all the problems of modern war.

∫

The beginnings of such a synthesis took shape after World War I. Successive reorganizations set up the staff divisions on a more realistic basis, and the function of planning for national industrial mobilization was made a responsibility of the War Department. Finally, in 1936, the status of the Chief of Staff was significantly clarified: he was, in peace, the commanding general of the field forces, and in war, he would continue to exercise field command until another commander was designated by the President. In 1941 the nation embarked on its second global conflict with a more efficient command system than in its first and one that was more in line with the American experience. These essays are not the proper medium to discuss the vast story of World War II or the elaborate command apparatus that emerged during that most global of all wars.[11] The theme is such as to defy treatment in a short space. But it is perhaps worthy of note that the British, at their first contact with our command system, were shocked at what they considered its ramshackle organization, one of them comparing the arrangements to those existing in George Washington's time. The British continued to be shocked at the way Franklin D. Roosevelt and other American leaders extemporized from day to day. Roosevelt improvised in war as he did in politics. Indeed, all the great American leaders have been essentially improvisers. Improvisation, as Elihu Root forgot, is a part of the American national genius and has been expressed in war as well as in other areas of national life.

After the war a tremendous reorganization of the military establishment was carried through in the National Security Acts of 1947 and 1949. Agencies were piled into superagencies that were supervised by superco-ordinating bodies. The elaborate new arrangements, so bewildering to the lay mind, were designed to enable the nation to deal with the ever increasing complexities of war. This postwar system has been subjected to strong criticism, including some by military men. It is, claim the critics, top-heavy, cumbersome, disjunctive, and inadequate for the requirements of modern war. Among the proposals advanced for reform have been the creation of a general staff aloof from the three services and with a

[11] The complexity of World War II command arrangements are summarized in William Emerson, "Franklin D. Roosevelt as Commander-in-Chief in World War II," *Military Affairs*, XXII (1958–59), 181–207.

single head, the relegation of the present Joint Chiefs of Staff to an advisory group, the formation of a separate combat command under the Secretary of Defense, and the establishment of a single service under a single commander.

These are problems that the historian does not have competence to solve. They are in the province of the political and military leaders and the specialists in administrative organization. But surely the historian has something of value to say to the men who will have to deal with these problems. He can tell them that a knowledge of American military history is important in itself. Some of the most serious shortcomings in our military policy have come about because soldiers and civilians have had an inadequate or inaccurate appreciation of our history. The historian can emphasize that no system will work well that breaks too sharply with the American past or ignores too much the American experience. And finally, he can remind his fellow countrymen that extemporized arrangements expressing the American spirit may be superior to blueprint charts, and—citing the examples of Washington, of Polk and Scott, and, above all, of Lincoln and Grant—he can show that men are vastly more significant than the structural perfection of any system.

Notes on Sources

IT IS DOUBTFUL if many historians who are so reckless as to write surveys of large themes could say from whence they drew all their materials. Certainly I could not locate accurately the source of every item in these essays dealing with high command in the American military experience. For approximately fifteen years I have taught a course in military history at Louisiana State University. During that period I have done some primary research in the area of the Civil War, and I have read widely in the published sources of the records of other wars. But necessarily, in attempting to reach the broad, and dangerous, plane of interpretation required in such a short study I have had to rely on many secondary works. The list which follows is intended to acknowledge my debt to the writers of these works and also to offer a guide to the reader who wishes to pursue the subject in more detail.

Basic for an understanding of the development of strategy is Edward M. Earle (ed.), *Makers of Modern Strategy* (Princeton, 1943). This admirable work, written by specialists in a variety of fields, reviews the history of strategic thinking from Machiavelli to Hitler. Another useful compendium, its broad content indicated by the title, is Gordon B. Turner (ed.), *A History of Military Affairs in Western Society Since the Eighteenth Century* (New York, 1952). No one book treats exclusively the theme of high command and high strategy in American history, but the main outlines of our military policy can be traced in a number of works. In *Arms and Men* (New York, 1956) Walter Millis describes the evolution of American military institutions and relates institutional developments to parallel social and economic forces in national life. Similar in content but less analytical is C. Joseph Bernardo and E. H. Bacon, *American Military Policy* (Harrisburg, 1955). The best study of staffs is J. D. Hittle, *The Military Staff* (Harrisburg, 1949). Dealing with the development of the general staff concept in the United States is Otto L. Nelson, *National Security and the General Staff* (Washington, 1946), which summarizes so many documents as to become in part a source account. Wholly documentary but containing valuable chunks of information is Raphael P. Thian (ed.), *Legislative History of the General Staff . . . from 1775 to 1901* (Washington, 1901). The history of naval policy is succinctly summarized in two books by Harold and Margaret Sprout: *The Rise of American Naval Power* (Princeton, 1939) and *Toward a New Order of Sea Power* (Princeton, 1940). The Sprouts were the first academic scholars to study seriously the story of naval policy. Their work is extremely valuable but colored by an undue admiration for the theories of Admiral Mahan.

In following institutional developments in the War Department, I have relied on the great history of administration by Leonard D. White: *The Federalists* (New York, 1948); *The Jeffersonians* (New York, 1951); *The Jacksonians* (New York, 1954); and *The Republican Era* (New York, 1958). This work by a political scientist, which truly deserves the label of monumental, should become an indispensable tool to historians. But while acknowledging my debt to Professor White, I must say, in self-protection, that I have traversed some of the same published sources as he, and in some cases I have resorted to the same quotations to illustrate particular points.

The history of the United States army has been written almost exclusively by military men. These soldier-authors have done good work, but understandably they have been influenced by their background and sometimes they have had particular viewpoints to stress. William A. Ganoe traces the army's record through World War I with accurate and often antiquarian detail in *The History of the United States Army* (New York, 1924). Similar in nature and carrying the story to the background of World War II is Oliver L. Spaulding, *The United States Army in War and Peace* (New York, 1937). Excellent on the origins of the army is James Ripley Jacobs, *The Beginning of the U.S. Army, 1783–1813* (Princeton, 1947). John McAuley Palmer describes the methods by which we have raised our armies in *America in Arms* (New Haven, 1941). General Palmer's little book is lively and challenging but marked by some special pleading. The author wanted to prove that a citizen army was our best defense, and he took direct issue with the case for a large professional army presented by General Emory Upton in *The Military Policy of the United States* (Washington, 1904). The most detailed study of mobilization is Marvin A. Kreidberg and Merton G. Henry, *History of Military Mobilization in the United States Army, 1775–1945* (Washington, 1955).

Except for the Civil War, more good writing has been done about the Revolution than any other of our conflicts. The following general accounts all give some attention to matters of strategy: John R. Alden, *The American Revolution, 1775–1783* (New York, 1954); Francis V. Greene, *The Revolutionary War and the Military Policy of the United States* (New York, 1911), especially good for its maps; Lynn Montross, *Rag, Tag and Bobtail: The Story of the Continental Army, 1776–1783* (New York, 1952);

Willard M. Wallace, *Appeal to Arms* (New York, 1951);
Christopher Ward, *The War of the Revolution* (2 vols.,
New York, 1952); and Howard H. Peckham, *The War for
Independence* (Chicago, 1958). The best account of the
war's greatest soldier is Douglas S. Freeman, *George Washington* (6 vols., New York, 1948–1954). John C. Miller
relates the reactions of members of the Continental Congress to Washington in *Triumph of Freedom, 1775–1783*
(Boston, 1948).

The unhappy War of 1812 has received scant attention
from historians. One of the best accounts, and undoubtedly the most acid, was presented by Henry Adams in his
multivolumed history of the administrations of Jefferson
and Madison. From this work H. A. DeWeerd extracted
the chapters dealing with the war and put them into a
single volume: Henry Adams, *The War of 1812* (Washington, 1944). Less positive and prejudiced and emphasiz-
ing the battles are Francis F. Beirne, *The War of 1812*
(New York, 1949) and Glenn Tucker, *Poltroons and
Patriots* (2 vols., Indianapolis, 1954). For the war at sea,
Alfred T. Mahan, *Seapower in its Relations to the War of
1812* (Boston, 1905), is still standard.

For the Mexican War there are a number of good works
available. The standard treatment is Justin H. Smith, *The
War with Mexico* (2 vols., New York, 1919). Most of the
facts are here, but some of the author's generalizations
should be accepted with caution. The best general account
is Robert S. Henry, *The Story of the Mexican War* (Indianapolis, 1950). Shorter but useful is Alfred H. Bill,
Rehearsal for Conflict (New York, 1947). Much of the
war, as well as of army history preceding it, is in two outstanding biographies of the conflict's leading soldiers:
Charles W. Elliott, *Winfield Scott* (New York, 1937) and
Holman Hamilton, *Zachary Taylor, Soldier of the Republic* (Indianapolis, 1941).

The Civil War has produced a massive historical literature, some of the items being among the best military history written in this country. But, surprisingly, only a few books of the thousands that have been written deal with the theme of high command and grand strategy. The first writers to treat the subject—and they did it well—were English soldiers: Colin R. Ballard, *The Military Genius of Abraham Lincoln* (London, 1926; new ed., Cleveland, 1952) and Sir Frederick Maurice, *Statesmen and Soldiers of the Civil War* (Boston, 1926). Another Englishman, General J. F. C. Fuller, brought out two books that challenged existing interpretations: *The Generalship of Ulysses S. Grant* (London, 1929; new ed., Bloomington, 1958) and *Grant and Lee* (London, 1933; new ed., Bloomington, 1957). General Fuller was one of the first writers to call attention to the greatness of Grant, and although he sometimes made his case too vehemently, he performed a scholarly service by attacking the romantic notion that the losers must have been the better generals. Other studies by British authors are B. H. Liddell Hart, *Sherman* (New York, 1929; new ed., New York, 1958), stimulating but often serving as a vehicle for the author's own strategic ideas, and A. H. Burne, *Lee, Grant and Sherman* (New York, 1939), a scholarly review of the campaigns of 1864–65. I have discussed the Northern command system in *Lincoln and His Generals* (New York, 1952), and Kenneth P. Williams describes army command relationships in *Lincoln Finds a General* (5 vols., New York, 1949–59). David Donald has an excellent essay on strategy in Chapter Five of his *Lincoln Reconsidered* (New York, 1956). For the Confederate side, Douglas S. Freeman analyzes strategy in the Eastern theater, without too much attention to the over-all picture, in *R. E. Lee* (4 vols., New York, 1949) and *Lee's Lieutenants* (3 vols., New York, 1942–44). The best general account of Confederate strategy is Frank Vandiver, *Rebel Brass* (Baton Rouge, 1956).

The work of the army after the Civil War has to be

traced in the reminiscences and biographies of such men as George Crook, George A. Custer, Charles King, and Nelson A. Miles, but it is most conveniently summarized in Fairfax Downey, *Indian-Fighting Army* (New York, 1941; new ed., New York, 1957). Adequate treatments of the Spanish-American War are scarce. Secretary of War Russell A. Alger gave his side of the story in *The Spanish-American War* (New York, 1901). Walter Millis presents a sparkling, if somewhat satiric, account in *The Martial Spirit* (Boston, 1931), and Frank Freidel gives us a pictorial record with a good narrative in *The Splendid Little War* (Boston, 1958). The best source for Secretary of War Root's ideas about military policy and army reforms is his own speeches and papers in Elihu Root, *The Military and Colonial Policy of the United States* (2 vols., Cambridge, 1916), compiled by Robert Bacon and James Scott.

It should be a matter of concern that no good history of World War I is available. The best general accounts, which are hardly adequate, are Frederic L. Paxson, *America at War, 1917–1918* (Boston, 1939) and Girard L. McEntee, *Military History of the World War* (New York, 1937). There is revealing material on the strategic thinking in the War Department in Frederick Palmer, *Newton D. Baker* (2 vols., New York, 1931). The two military protagonists of the war stated their case in memoirs: Peyton C. March, *The Nation at War* (New York, 1932) and John J. Pershing, *My Experiences in the World War* (2 vols., New York, 1931). Also useful are the following personal narratives: Robert L. Bullard, *Personalities and Reminiscences of the War* (New York, 1925); Johnson Hagood, *The Services of Supply* (Boston, 1927); James G. Harbord, *America in the World War* (Boston, 1933) and *The American Army in France* (Boston, 1936); and Hunter Liggett, *Commanding an American Army* (Boston, 1925).

Already the vast experience of World War II has been

responsible for a respectable body of literature, whose extent can only be indicated here. Personal narratives, biographies, and studies of particular campaigns have poured from the presses in the United States and foreign countries. Satisfactory introductory accounts are Cyril Falls, *The Second World War* (London, 1948); J. F. C. Fuller, *The Second World War* (New York, 1949); and Chester Wilmot, *The Struggle for Europe* (New York, 1952). Perhaps the most significant historical development coming out of the war was the decision of the three services to have the story of their participation compiled by trained historians. Completed under the editorship of Wesley F. Craven and James L. Cate is *The Army Air Forces in World War II* (7 vols., Chicago, 1948–58). Samuel Eliot Morison has finished twelve volumes of *History of Naval Operations in World War II* (Boston, 1947–58); two more volumes are scheduled to appear. From the viewpoint of sheer size the most impressive service project is the *United States Army in World War II*, prepared by the Office of the Chief of Military History. Approximately ninety volumes are planned, of which some thirty have been published. The following deal particularly with problems of command: Mark S. Watson, *Chief of Staff: Prewar Plans and Preparations* (1950); Maurice Matloff and Edwin M. Snell, *Strategic Planning for Coalition Warfare* (1953); and Forrest C. Pogue, *The Supreme Command* (1954). The crucial strategic decisions of the war are summarized in Samuel Eliot Morison, *Strategy and Compromise* (Boston, 1958).

In the decade and a half since 1945 tremendous changes in weapons development have taken place, altering drastically the nature of warfare. Probably no other period of history has witnessed so many technological innovations in so short a space of time. The result has been to arouse doubt in the minds of some that our present military organization is adequate to cope with the problems of modern war. A substantial literature of criticism has appeared, some of it purely polemical, some of it deeply thoughtful. The reader who wishes to venture into this controversial area may find enlightenment in the following works: Thomas K. Finletter, *Power and Policy* (New York, 1954), a plea for air power; Henry A. Kissinger, *Nuclear Weapons and Foreign Policy* (New York, 1957), an argument for flexibility in weapons; Sir John Slessor, *Strategy for the West* (New York, 1954), which recognizes both the capabilities and limitations of air power; and James M. Gavin, *War and Peace in the Space Age* (New York, 1958), the reflections of an army officer not in entire agreement with official policy. In *The Armor of Organization* (New York, 1953) Alvin Brown attacks the staff concept and recommends a new plan of organization for the military system.

Index